THE
HEALING
POWER
OF
TREES

Giacomo Tosti

About the Author

Sharlyn Hidalgo, MA, has been a practicing astrologer, dream interpreter, and tarot reader for more than twenty-five years. She teaches classes on the Egyptian Mysteries and the Celtic tree calendar, is a certified practitioner and teacher of Alchemical Healing, and has worked as a counselor in agencies and in private practice. Visit her blog at www.alchemicalhealingarts.blogspot.com.

THE
HEALING
POWER
OF
TREES

SPIRITUAL JOURNEYS
THROUGH THE
CELTIC TREE CALENDAR

SHARLYN
HIDALGO

Llewellyn Publications
Woodbury, Minnesota

Cover design by Lisa Novak
Cover illustration by Meraylah Allwood
Editing by Laura Graves
Interior illustrations by Meraylah Allwood,
    except pages 20 and 221 by Llewellyn art department

Llewellyn is a registered trademark of Llewellyn Worldwide Ltd.

Note: This book is not meant to substitute for the advice of a licensed professional. This book is sold with the understanding that the author and publisher are not engaged in rendering medical or health services. The author and publisher expressly disclaim all responsibility for any liability, loss, risk, or injury resulting from the use and application of any of the contents of this book.

ISBN 978-0-7387-1998-6

Llewellyn Publications
A Division of Llewellyn Worldwide Ltd.
2143 Wooddale Drive
Woodbury, MN 55125-2989

Printed in the United States of America

*This book is dedicated to my children,
my nieces and nephews, and their children,
who carry on the dreams and aspirations
of our ancestors from the British Isles.*

The oak and the pines, and their brethren of the wood, have seen so many suns rise and set, so many seasons come and go, and so many generations pass into silence, that we may well wonder what "the story of the trees" would be to us if they had tongues to tell, or we ears fine enough to understand.

AUTHOR UNKNOWN,
quoted in *Quotations for Special Occasions*
by Maud Van Buren, 1938

CONTENTS

• The Celtic Tree Calendar •

NGETAL · REED
September 5—October 2
149

STRAIF · BLACKTHORN
September 5—October 2 (Same as Ngetal/Reed)
159

RUIS · ELDER
October 3—30
167

THE DAY
October 31
177

· Appendices ·

AILIM · SILVER FIR/PINE
189

OHN · GORSE/FURZE
192

UR · HEATHER/MISTLETOE
194

EADHA · WHITE POPLAR/ASPEN
196

IOHO · YEW
198

THE KOAD · THE GROVE
201

OIR · SPINDLE
205

UILLEAND · HONEYSUCKLE
207

PHAGOS · BEECH
210

MOR · THE SEA
213

ACKNOWLEDGMENTS

I began this journey out of a deep desire for connection with spirit. I did not know how to do this, yet I followed an intuitive thread towards my own heritage from the British Isles. I chose books that might inform me. I held ceremonies that honored the full moon for a year, then the new moon for a year, and then the Celtic holidays for a year. Finally, I took on the ceremonies for each month of the Celtic tree calendar. I am so grateful to the men and women who came to my ceremonies and classes. I taught what I hoped to learn about, and I received more than I could have ever imagined. My greatest gift came as a knowing in my bones that other dimensions of love and light are available to us. I have experienced and seen miracles.

I am grateful to my many teachers, especially Starfeather, Starhawk, Diane Stein, Brooke Medicine Eagle, Vicki Noble, Danielle Rama Hoffman, Ffiona Morgan, Barbara Walker, Zsuzsanna Budapest, and Nicki Scully. I want to thank my very first little circle with Beth Johns, Alice Quintance, and Margery Hite. Thank you to Gloria Taylor Brown and her channeling of Thoth, which prompted me to complete this book and get it to my publisher.

I want to thank my husband, Ricardo Hidalgo, and my children, Eli (Cairn) Werner-Limardi and Rianna Hidalgo, for their willingness to share our home so that I could teach classes and run ceremonies.

This was no small sacrifice on their part. I want to thank all of my incredible nieces for their love and support as well.

I want to thank my first women's circle who met monthly for years: Nancy, Karen, Linda Sue, Deborah, Gina, Jennifer, Donna, and Willa. Thanks to my healing circle of Maxine, Colleen, Karen, Starfeather, Maggie, and Teresa. I am grateful to the men and women who came to my Celtic holiday ceremonies. Thanks too to the friends, acquaintances, and students who came to my tree circles, and thank you to all the women who attended my workshops in California, Oregon, and Seattle.

I want to thank Julia Adame, Connie Vierling, Jennifer McClure, Starfeather, Beth Johns, Karen Johansen, Willa Werner, and Sandy Nisley-Leader for their continual support and encouragement over the years. And I offer gratitude to my new friends and students and co-healers within the Alchemical Healing Community here in Seattle.

I am especially grateful to the tools of my trade: the tarot cards, astrology, the runes, and the healing arts of Alchemical Healing™ and Huna. I am grateful to the totems of Crone, Bear, Eagle, and Dolphin for all of their special teaching. And finally I thank my ancestors who once lived on the British Isles in the midst of woods and forests, long since gone…thank you for this system of knowledge you have passed down through eons.

I especially want to thank the powerful healing of Hathor's Sycamore tree that stands at the entrance to the temple of Ptah, Sekhmet, and Nefertum at the Karnak temple in Luxor, Eygpt. Thank you for the words I heard in Seti I's tomb in the Valley of the Kings, "Oh, it is the tree lady. Welcome!" This was a surprising encouragement! Here I experienced the light and love of who I am. This was not a place of death at all, but a blueprint for becoming.

Thank you for my personal symbol of the tree and the cup and the words "Ancient Sovereignty" given to me by my ancestors from the British Isles while in a guided visualization. Thank you to the Atlantians and Thoth for making sure wisdom and the principles of nature were given to the lands of Ireland, Wales, Scotland, and Britain. Lastly, thank you to the trees themselves for the wealth of teaching and magic support. I honor them and give my gratitude.

INTRODUCTION

The trees are especially powerful in their healing energies. It is for this reason, and because of my ancestry, that I follow the Celtic tree calendar based on the thirteen moon months of the year. It is in this way that I stay close to the natural world and Universal Intelligence and Love; Goddess, God, and all that is!

In the Celtic tradition, it is said there were originally two powerful source energies that came to our planet through the first rays of the sun, long before humans appeared. These energies were called *Celi* and *Cerridwen*—male and female—and they embodied the laws of the universe (the macrocosm) and the laws of the natural world (the microcosm). Celi and Cerridwen spread their knowledge and essence in the form of spirits called *dryads*. Dryads became the keepers of the original creators' teachings and made their homes in the trees.

Each sacred tree of the dryads represented a cosmic expression of this primeval archetypal essence, which later became associated with Celtic gods and goddesses and formed the rich fabric of Celtic story and myth. There are twenty-five trees, runes, and Celtic ogham letters that represent the teachings of these dryads. Fifteen of these trees are part of the Celtic tree calendar. The tree alphabet was used in the British Isles from approximately 600 BCE until about AD 700 (Murray and Collins, 7–8).

The essence of the early spiritual practices of the British Isles embraces and supports natural law and order, of which we as humans are an important part. In order to establish and maintain our correct place as stewards in the cosmos, I believe we can reclaim what was once ours. I believe many of us are hungry and ready for guidance as we work toward changing and uplifting our consciousness.

Most spiritual paths lead pupils through developmental stages of consciousness. Disciples are led through these stages through initiations. In a manner of speaking, we are ripe for what has been preserved and protected in the various mystery schools of our world. It is my belief that by returning to ancient systems of knowledge and using them in our daily lives, we can support and encourage the changes required on all levels that will preserve our species and our beautiful planet. This is not to say we can go back to purely ancient ways, but we can connect with these teachings to receive guidance from source that can enable us to live in the present and meet our challenges.

Celtic tradition and culture honored the wisdom of the earth. Women were honored as healers and midwives. The cycles of the sun and the moon were honored as well. The Celts learned about the power of the plants and trees to heal. They prayed to the elements, the animals, the trees, and the rocks. All held essence and spirit and teaching. Reverence and gratitude were part and parcel of everyday life. Contact with unseen worlds was taken for granted, and magic was developed out of knowledge given through communication with other dimensions. Shamanism was not out of the ordinary.

With foreign invasion of the British Isles came imposed cultural, political, and religious beliefs that attempted to end the indigenous way of harmonious life with the laws of nature. Other traditions and religious beliefs curtailed ancient ways, but did not completely kill them. The infusion of Christianity brought crucial change. Many people, including women, were burned at the stake as witches. People were labeled as heretics and were persecuted. The Catholic Church and its grand inquisition, as well as the Protestant churches, did a masterful job of creating fear and repression. The knowledge went underground but did not die.

Today, we are beginning to respect and learn about the spiritual knowledge of ancient cultures and understand that indigenous people carry the keys to the very survival of our planet. Native European people have much in common with the Native Americans and other indigenous peoples worldwide. People on the North American and European continents developed rich traditions of myth and legend passed on through generations. Celtic knowledge is one such mystery school available to us, and through it we can understand and appreciate our true nature. We can look to these spiritual sensibilities to steady us in the intense times in which we live. We can look to the ancient wisdom as a way to increase our consciousness and identify as spiritual beings. We can reaffirm our interconnectedness with all life.

As Great Britain was deforested, her people lost their connection to nature, a great tragedy not given much thought today. If we reclaim the knowledge that was lost and bring it forward to unite with this time and this place, we can create something new. The spirits of the British Isles welcome this new synergy. Considering the destruction of the earth at this present time (for which our species is responsible), returning to ancient wisdom that embodies natural law is essential. If we can survive the next ten or fifteen years without blowing ourselves up and harming our planet beyond repair, our beliefs, behaviors, feelings, and actions will evolve and this may help to ensure our peace and harmony. We can understand with reverence and humility that we are powerful co-creators with source. We can create a world we wish to live in that gives proper respect to all life forms.

I've had a longtime desire to reconnect with my true place and position in the grand scheme of things; it has motivated me to dig into my own ancestral past. I have spent years interacting with and sharing these teachings, and my connection with the archetypal power that rests in the trees has changed my life. I hope that in bringing these teachings forward that others can use them for encouragement, support, and meaning. I hope we all can reconnect with our birthright, and joyfully take up our responsibility as stewards of our incredible paradise.

THE TREES'
ESSENTIAL ROLE

The truth is, we could not live without trees. Trees act as our planet's lungs. Trees take in the carbon dioxide we exhale, and we breathe in the oxygen they "exhale"; we have a mutually beneficial relationship. They do us a great service of cleaning our air as well, and without them, our atmosphere would become impossibly toxic to us.

They also are responsible for drawing water into the soil, essential to the water cycle that provides drinkable groundwater. Trees also release water into the atmosphere, allowing for the condensation that causes rain. Without the rain, desertification begins. This leads to massive famines as the topsoil is blown away. The evaporation leaf surface of a single tree is equivalent to the evaporation of a forty-acre lake (Hartmann, 42).

As we destroy the forests that provide us with these essential ecological cornerstones, we have fewer oxygen-releasing leaf surfaces, less circulation in the water cycle, and increased desertification, while we continue to burn trees and place more carbon into the atmosphere. It seems we have no concept of the trees' essential role in our ecosystems. Forests are imperiled worldwide. We are not connected to nature enough to realize that when the forests are in danger, we are too.

Trees also grant us source knowledge and essence. Trees stand upright, as we do; their trunks are like our bodies, their limbs like arms, their roots like legs. They stand between Mother Earth and Father Sky, as we do. We are both grand bridges between these two spheres of consciousness. They mirror to us our own pattern of spiritual awareness and knowing that travels from our roots that connect us to the earth on up to our crown, connecting us to all that is above. This inner spiritual structure is called the *djed,* the tree of knowledge. It is this inner tree that has been given to our species, a gift that is mirrored in the function of all trees and what we spiritually share with actual trees. As Celtic tradition teaches, each tree species embodies its own knowledge. We can tune in to tree wisdom and converse with it. Our tree teachers are available to us all; we only have to sit with a tree and listen.

The mystery of consciousness is what allows us to evolve, and our evolution is intimately intertwined with trees. Our stewardship, then, is our heritage and our true purpose. The trees are here to remind us of our duty. They call to us and say:

"We are healers. You are healers. All life is sacred, as is our connection to you and you to us. Wake up, humankind, and take up your rightful place and heritage in the holy scheme of nature. We are not separate and have never been so. Paradise exits right here and right now. Paradise is this planet in its beauty and perfection. We invite you to become one with us and recognize the perfection that you are and that we are. Remember, in protecting the tree people, you are protecting your own species and all of life. This is what you are to do. This is your stewardship."

MY STORY

The Apple Tree and the Cedar Tree

I feel very blessed that an apple tree saved my life. My apple tree healing occurred in 1982; I was thirty-five. At that time, my life was very stressful and demanding; I was a new parent, and my marriage, which should have been my solid foundation, was crumbling and unstable. Hopelessness, inadequacy, and anxiety seemed to be the only feelings I had. In a very black and despondent mood (yes, thoughts of suicide), I cried out for help and found myself running into the arms of a huge apple tree that beckoned me from the vacant lot behind my house.

I wrapped my arms around the tree, and to my utter amazement, the tree responded! Its response was visceral: it was unconditionally loving, reassuring, and the most wonderful sort of energizing. I was startled out of my despair and completely taken aback: was I crazy? Did I make this up? The impression I was left with was one of a communication of help, comfort, and encouragement—the tree's perfect gift. My mood lifted, and I was smiling. I went back to my job of being a wife and mother as best I could. Years later, while studying the Celtic tree calendar, I discovered the apple tree's association with choice as well as beauty. Indeed, both these lessons reached me on that life-changing day. I am forever grateful for her lessons.

I began a new relationship with, and found a new understanding of, trees as healers and communicators after receiving the apple tree's message. Curious for more, I looked at all the trees around me, and became more aware them, grateful for their presence. I also began New Age and Eastern religious studies. I began to understand things differently and interacted with nature's unseen realms. While working as a teacher for high school dropout students, I developed my skills as a tarot reader and astrologer, and fostered the strong guidance I received from dreams.

Time passed, and my life changed again radically. I divorced, went back to school, received my master's in psychology, eventually remarried, had a daughter, and started working as a part-time therapist. I was so involved in the workings of everyday life that it wasn't until my late forties that I realized I needed spiritual renewal in my life.

I was ready and able to attend to my own soul. I made a commitment to myself to pursue a spiritual path that would feed me. My path brought me back to the trees. Simply, I asked the universe to supply me with what I needed. I decided to abandon traditional religion and remain open to what would bring me true spiritual rejuvenation.

The first teaching that came to me was through Brooke Medicine Eagle's *Buffalo Woman Comes Singing* and a woman named Starfeather, who held drumming circles in her suburban home. In Starfeather's circle, I found a spiritual connection and learned the power of my own voice, the drum, and music to break down walls of separation and fear. Drumming made my soul sing and I felt happy, but I couldn't always make the drive to Starfeather's house; sometimes family life took precedence. I still wanted—needed—that spiritual connectedness, ceremony, and experience, so I decided to have my own circles at home. I very much wanted to continue to attend Starfeather's circles; I loved them, and loved her leadership. I had no desire to become a circle leader, but out of my intense need I was willing to become one.

Starfeather also led pipe ceremonies, which followed Native American tradition in a sacred and beautiful way. Through these, I received my second teaching: a sense of missing home. I don't mean I missed my house in Seattle; what I experienced was a deep homesickness for another way of being in circle, my own native European roots as expressed through the Celtic tradition. I began my own Celtic circles in town, a women's group that performed many ceremonies based on ancient European earth religion and the full and new moons. I started working with Celtic holidays and taught classes. Through these activities, I found the wholeness I was searching for, and finally began to understand my life's purpose.

It was during this period that my family moved to a new house with two huge old cedar trees in the yard that offered many blessings: protection, shade, cleansing, clean oxygen, beauty, and wisdom. The cedars attracted all kinds of wildlife, and it was always a pleasure to look outside and see blue jays, crows, squirrels, raccoons, and even owls and eagles come to my trees.

I honored these two trees as much as I could, but after eight years, wanted to move somewhere in the country where I could be even closer to the forest. I sold my house to a couple who were interested in having the property declared a natural protected habitat. It was the least I could give to them in return for all their healing.

I didn't expect that these trees would continue to bless me, but they did. While reading tarot cards at a Women of Wisdom Conference in Seattle, a palm reader (who also did Reiki) and I were able to come to the aid of a cook who was preparing a huge banquet; she was threatened by a migraine and was afraid she wouldn't be able to finish dinner for everyone. To my surprise, I immediately saw and heard the cedars in my mind's eye, and began to channel information on as I was told. The other woman was to apply Reiki to our patient's head, and I led us all through a guided meditation in which the woman was to imagine the cedar's healing sap slowly trickling from her head down to her feet like honey. She was able to feel this. Then, our patient was to imagine growing rootsdown into the Mother Earth and release the sap there. At the same time, she was told that she could begin to draw up light energy and sustenance from the earth. All her tension, fear, worry, and negative emotions were released. Calmness, joy, and light were retrieved through the root system back into the woman's whole body, and even into her aura. I was told to place my hands on her feet the entire time, to help activate the flow of energy down and out, and then to encourage the Earth energy back up to rejuvenate her. The healing worked, and the joyful and relieved woman was able to continue her job.

After these powerful tree experiences, I began studying the Celtic tree calendar and holding monthly ceremonies that honored one tree each month. I also opened up to the idea that I too was a healer.

I was on a mission: I felt compelled to learn as much as I could about the Celtic tree calendar without really understanding my motivation. I know I felt happier and inspired when I did so. I know I felt plugged into magic, beauty, and peace. There was positive energy and a connection offered to me. New totems, guides, and deities showed up in guided meditations to share teachings and healings. The trees themselves offered me guidance and nourishment.

Trees will share with you, too. It is so easy to some time with a tree and just listen. Starfeather and other wonderfully gifted women compiled a presentation of songs for the trees, and Starfeather's words are imprinted upon my heart: "When we know that the trees are sacred, we will stop cutting them down." It is my thought that when we know that we are sacred as well, we will stop killing each other and unite, as the true stewards we are, to protect and preserve all life forms upon the planet. This is my message, desire, and hope. It is my "intuitive directive," if you will, that tree knowledge may help us understand that we are sacred. It is also my desire that we will gain the knowledge and proof we need to understand that we are just as important as the trees are to the preservation of all that is.

Our ability to experience this connection is the key factor in waking up to this great physical reality in which we are taking part. We are creating our reality and we have so much help. The paradise in which we live needs us to rediscover this connection so that we can once again become the stewards we were meant to be. When we can experience the sacredness in ourselves, we will honor the sacredness of our planet. When we experience the connection between what occurs within us to what occurs outside of us, we begin to understand our responsibility. We are the microcosm of the macrocosm. And we are co-creators "dying" to become awake. Blessed be; enjoy the book; welcome home. You live in paradise, and you are awesome already!

HOW TO USE THIS BOOK

This book will provide you with introductory information about the Celtic tree calendar and the Celtic cosmology. You will be introduced to the runes, the ogham, astrology, Celtic mythology, and the particular tree teachings. You will discover many totems, guides, and deities. This book serves as a doorway into these topics and is a wonderful source for your studies. For a broader overview, you can read the entire book once and go back for more in-depth study.

That being said, this book is not meant to be a meticulous research of these topics. I took what I found and made it my own. I used the information so I could interface with the true nature of the world and expand my own experience of the universe. By opening up to the unseen realms, I have been blessed with a greater sense of awe and connection. Hopefully this will be true for you as well.

This book will lead you to actual experiences with the trees. You will be energetically rewarded for any time or attention you give. You can use each month's description for a particular tree and sit with it, gather leaves, berries, fruit, bark, and twigs, and bring its energy into your environment. You can gather pictures of the tree and its particular totems and guides, and you can read more about the Celtic deities in Celtic stories and legends. For instance, I like to read about Bran and Branwen during the Alder month. Reading about these deities makes them come alive for me.

I know when I first became interested in the trees I had to research them on the Internet, find books at the library, and begin to identify them in my neighborhood and local parks. I asked people to help me identify them wherever I could. Every time I discovered a new tree, I felt encouraged and kept adding to my tree repertoire.

As you go through the book, place the tree name at the beginning tree date of each tree month on a blank calendar. Begin with November 1 so you know which tree is the lord or master over the month, and use the calendar to go through that particular tree chapter. Play with the ogham, rune, and astrology. Keep the portal's healing properties in mind as you go through the month and experiment with the teachings, meditation, and healings. See what happens and discover how tree energy supports your life. Go through the book month by month. You can begin with the current month and spend it with that tree chapter, but I suggest beginning with Birch, the Celtic New Year. Doing so will move you through the dark and light halves of the year in a more harmonious way.

Each month, try to find and spend time with its tree and other trees you enjoy. If you can't find a particular tree in your local environment, be willing to exchange it for the energy of a tree you know. Take time to be quiet and listen. If I can't get outside to a tree, I make time for inner meditation and picture a tree in my mind to be with. For instance, when I am in need of strength and grounding, I picture a huge oak tree. When beginning new projects, I call on Birch. When I am unable to physically visit a tree, I use my mind's eye to sit under the tree and tap into its energy for ten or so minutes. The tree often has a message or an encouraging word and speaks to me internally. See what tree shows up for you when you sit quietly, and intend to communicate. Guides, totems, and deities often show up to be part of a meditation.

Attending to the Wheel of the Year and celebrating the many holidays is a joyful way to go through the year. This is a good structure for planning either independent ritual or group ceremony. This book offers guided meditations that can be used in ceremonies. I took information I researched and planned rituals, meditation, and ceremonies that ended up being fun and life altering. I encourage you to do the same. Use this book to plan your own ceremonies, retreats, gatherings, teachings, and explorations. Creative use of your energies can only benefit and enrich you.

Each tree goes with a lunation and falls within the thirteen moon months of the year, so the lunar influence is important. Keep your eye on the moon and notice when it is waxing and waning, and when it is new and full. Keeping track of the moon is an important way to keep in touch with nature. Notice the path of the moon in the night sky during whatever month you are studying. Paying attention will bring you into a working rhythm with that month's tree.

Take the guided meditations in the book as part of your inner work. Journeying or pathworking requires using your imagination. Through pathworking, you can align yourself with the energies of deities and mythic figures. A guided journey takes you into the inner world of the universal, archetypal, and astral planes such that you may acquire lasting change on an unconscious (or subconscious) level. It is a good idea to have someone read the journey to you, or you can record it ahead of time to enter into the journey more easily. Adding music to help you deepen your experience can be wonderful as long as it is not too sad- or violent-sounding. People often ask, "Am I just making this up?" I would say if you are, it's not a problem. You are using the right side of your brain to connect with your subconscious, and it does not care if what you experience is "real" or not—it is willing to play along and will respond. Use your senses of feeling, imagining, sensing, seeing, or smelling to enrich your journey. You will be amazed at the riches that lie silently within you ready to communicate love and wisdom.

I suggest you purchase or make your own special journal for recording your journeys and experiences. Coming out of a guided meditation is basically coming out of a light trance, and it is easy to forget details, much like when you wake up from a dream. You can dedicate your book to the trees and keep a section for each of the fifteen trees. After a year of study and journeying, you will be amazed at how you have changed in a positive way, though ultimately, you get back what you put in.

People are often surprised at the healing that takes place in these journeys as one turns to their internal space. It is this "within" territory where we truly find our answers. When you need a particular healing, refer to the section for each tree and its healing offerings. The more you experiment, the more you will reap each tree's benefits. Consulting the trees will create a huge paradigm shift for you, as your mundane way of viewing reality will change.

You can also use this book as an oracle: ask your questions or state your concerns and open to a page. It may direct you to use the runes or ogham, or to look further into a particular tree's message. Make your own tree cards or ogham sticks. What you use will be especially helpful as a teaching tool, and you will develop your own intuition as you play with the meanings and portals each represents. Get a set of runes or make your own. I drew each rune on little stones and used them as a divination tool, and I made my own tree cards.

You might choose to use my own personal stories as a pattern for how you can communicate with the trees. My own experiences can encourage you to find solace with the trees and to seek transmission of positive life-force energy from these grand, energetic, and loving beings. If it can happen for me, it is available to us all—I am not too different from you, the reader!

I believe it was out of my personal need at crucial difficult times in my life that the trees responded to me. They offered me help and solace long before I was able to understand their incredible gifts. It was really individual trees that sought me out. I know that the more determined I became to cultivate relationships with the trees, the more I was rewarded and my life enriched. I also experienced the feelings of love and growth anytime I focused on a totem, guide, priestess, or deity. As you work with a particular tree month, you will notice synchronicities, dreams, and waking situations that respond to and reinforce your studies. The unseen world is full of riches and delights to encourage you as you expand your consciousness and become more enlightened through your connection to nature.

I do not claim that this information is historically accurate or that my ancestors believed everything in this book to the letter. However, I have taken what I have found and made it useful in my life. The power and love within nature and the unseen realms, along with the power of my own rich imagination, has infused my life with meaning and joy. My connection to the trees is real, and I hope it will be for you too. Use this book as a system to support your spiritual nature. It is not a religion, nor is it a doctrine. This book and its teachings are a doorway through which you can commingle with the powerful principles of nature to navigate a sacred and responsible life filled with magic and mystery.

As a last note, I wrote this book for whoever is interested: it is meant for people of anyone, regardless of gender. If you are a man, please change the language to fit you. You can include gods and male guides within the meditations and ceremonies—Celtic mythology has quite a few. When I wrote many of the meditations, I was working mainly with women, but many holiday celebrations included both sexes. When I first did a ceremony for each tree, sometimes only women attended, and other times, men joined as well. I've changed the language of a meditation or ceremony to fit the circumstance and to be inclusive. It is not my intention to exclude anyone.

I hope this book will inspire you to give gratitude to the trees and the unseen world. Gratitude and attention is your payment as you enter the portals of these helpful energies. I hope you will find ways each month (or year) to give back to the trees.

What Is the Celtic Ogham Alphabet?

The *ogham* is the name given to the symbols and letters of the Celtic tree alphabet; it's pronounced "owam" or "ohm."

The alphabet is made up of symbols of straight lines that can be etched upon sticks or stone. Each symbol represents a particular letter and can be written vertically (usually read from bottom to top) or horizontally (usually read from left to right). An arrow shaft or some other kind of marking will usually indicate where to begin reading. The markings are made along a stem line called the *druim,* or the "whale's backbone." This alphabet was not use for writing or speech as we know it, but was used to indicate ideas and beliefs related to Celtic cosmology and philosophy. The ogham was often scratched onto stone or wooden staves.

There are twenty-five letters within this alphabet; each is named after a tree or plant, or after a natural element such as lightning or the sea. Legend says these letters were inspired by Ogmu, the god of eloquence who has ties to Thoth and Hermes or Mercury, also gods of communication and writing. Ogmu represents the archetype of our higher wisdom and intellect.

Ogham letters are arranged in five groups of five letters. The first twenty letters are called the *feada,* or fews, and are the original characters. These first four groups are referred to as the *aicme,* meaning "tribes," and are probably symbolic of Ireland's provinces. The first fifteen are the consonants and are comprised of the first five, called the *Aicme Beith*; the second five called the *Aicme hÚatha*; and the third five, called the *Aicme Muine.* The next five are the vowel groups, and they are known as the *Aicme Ailim.*

The last five are called the *forfeda* or the "Crane Bag" and are said to have been a gift from the sea god Manannan. These add a special significance of wisdom to this belief system. The forfeda represent the vowel combinations as well as consonant combinations. Because they are more complex, they could not have easily been carved on sticks and stone. These are said to have been added to the alphabet later to accommodate Greek and Latin.

Much of our present-day knowledge of the ogham comes from the *Book of Ballimore,* written in the fourteenth century. George Calder from the University of Glasgow published a book entitled *Auraicept na n'Eces,* or *The Scholar's Primer,* which transcribes this early material (Murray and Collins, 16). Other early manuscripts, such as the Book of Lecan, the Book of Lismore, and the Book of Leinster, also mention the ogham (Kynes, 41).

In addition to the actual writing of the ogham symbols, the hand was used to represent the letters. Finger and hand movements could be used to communicate the alphabet. (See the hand diagram on the next page, showing which fingers and knuckles represented which letters.) Thus, the druids had a nonverbal hand language known only to initiates, and its secrecy was possibly one way the alphabet was kept alive over time in spite of various invasions and the eventual repression of pagan beliefs. There were other forms of this communication system, known as the shinbone ogham and the nose ogham, in which the fingers could be placed upon the shin or nose to communicate.

Another way the letters were arranged was upon a sacred doorway called a dolmen. These were prehistoric structures of stone, a large flat stone laid across two upright ones. The dolmen represented a bridge between this world and the underworld, and served as a threshold into other realms. Standing stones are all over the British Isles, many with ogham and rune inscriptions.

It is thought that druids developed the ogham system, although its origins were probably from even earlier times in the history of the British Isles. Druids were wise elders who established powerful positions as advisors to tribal leaders and developed a unique relationship with nature. Through careful observations of the cycles and rhythms of nature, these special people developed a unique cosmology and followed a system of ritual and ceremony which honored the trees and celestial bodies' movements in their annual cycles.

The druids developed and used many techniques for divination. They used birds, weather, and the trees to divine the future. It is said that the ogham themselves were originally developed from the observations of the different leg movements of the crane in flight. The ogham alphabet and the special teachings and principles it embodied were taught through question and answer and passed on through memorization.

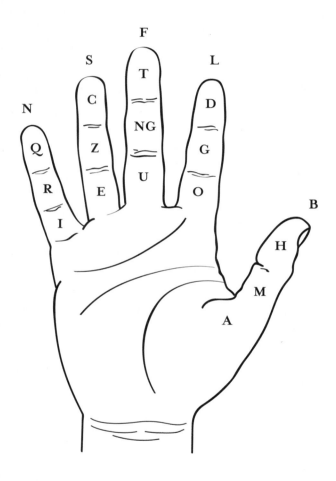

The first twenty ogham are called the feada:

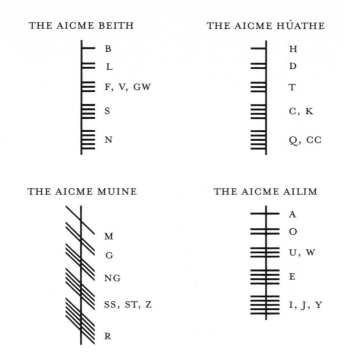

THE AICME BEITH

B
L
F, V, GW
S
N

THE AICME HÚATHE

H
D
T
C, K
Q, CC

THE AICME MUINE

M
G
NG
SS, ST, Z
R

THE AICME AILIM

A
O
U, W
E
I, J, Y

The last five ogham are called the forfeda:

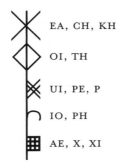

EA, CH, KH

OI, TH

UI, PE, P

IO, PH

AE, X, XI

The Ogham

The ogham can be read vertically or horizontally along a stem line. Horizontal lines are usually read from left to right, and they start where there is a V shape or some other marker. A dot is used to indicate the end of a word. Vertical lines are usually read from bottom to top.

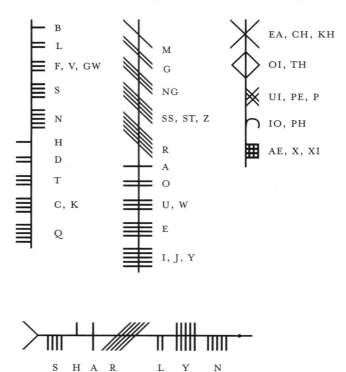

The author's name is written in ogham. Try writing your name. You can make your own set of ogham and use them as a divination tool. Gather sticks and cut them about the same size. Remove the bark, perhaps sand and paint them, and write the letters and ogham on them with perhaps a few words that show their significance. Popsicle sticks work well. Ogham cards can easily be made and are a fun, creative endeavor. I have made my own cards as a learning tool and found that they were good teachers. I also draw one card each day as a divination tool and as a way of focusing my energy.

The Feada
(the fews)

⊢	⊨	⊨	⊨	⊨
BEITH Birch Beginnings	**LUIS** Rowan Protection Astral Travel	**FEARN** Alder Guidance	**SAILLE** Willow Feminine Principle Intuition	**NUIN** Ash World Tree Inner/Outer
⊣	⊣	⊣	⊣	⊣
HUATHE Hawthorn Cleansing	**DUIR** Oak Strength	**TINNE** Holly Justice Lovers Polarity	**COLL** Hazel Intuition Wisdom	**QUERT** Apple Choice Ancestors Gaia
⅄	⅄	⅄	⅄	⅄
MUIN Vine Prophecy Ecstasy	**GORT** Ivy Labyrinth Journey into Self	**NGETAL** Reed Direct Action	**STRAIF** Blackthorn Negation	**RUIS** Elder Death Rebirth
+	╪	≡	≣	≣
AILIM Silver Fir Foresight Higher Vision	**OHN** Gorse/Furze Collecting Gathering	**UR** Heather Healing Spiritual Power	**EADHA** Poplar/Aspen Adversity Courage	**IOHO** Yew Rebirth Legacies Ancients

The Forfeda
(the extra fews)

✳	◇	⋉	ℎ	⊞
THE KOAD The Grove/ Temple Silence Meditation The Void	**OIR** Spindle Fulfillment Insight Light Lightning	**UILLEAND** Honeysuckle Secrets Seeking Insight	**PHAGOS** Beech Generations Past Knowledge	**MOR** The Sea Journeys Maternal Links The Land

What Are the Runes?

The runes are a system of symbols used for divination or guidance. They are an ancient alphabetic script. Each letter represented a special name and sound and, like the ogham, was not a spoken language. Runic symbols were used in legal documents, poetry, inscriptions, and divinations (Blum, 12).

The runes are said to originally have come from Germany, Scandinavia, and Iceland. They were probably brought to the British Isles through Nordic invasions by the Vikings. The influence of these runes is found in Anglo-Saxon England, where runic standing stones can still be found.

According to legend, it was Odin, the major god of the Norse people, who was gifted with this runic knowledge. He suffered for nine days and nine nights, hung from the great central Tree of the World called Yggdrasil. Reminiscent of the Hanged Man of the tarot, Odin's sacrifice and ordeal brought forth the runes through vision, granted to him by the three female fates.

I have included the runes as an accompaniment to the divination quality of the ogham and the trees. In my experience, they add to the information presented, are an amazing oracle, and provide unique guidance. They also represent another tie to the ancestors of the British Isles who used them.

The Twenty-Five Runes

1. **B** — Berkano/Growth

2. **ᚱ** — Laguz/Flow

3. **ᚠ** — Fehu/Possessions

4. **ᛋ** — Sowelo/Wholeness

5. **ᚾ** — Naudhiz/Constraint

6. **H** — Hagalaz/Disruption

7. **ᛞ** — Daguz/Breakthrough

8. **↑** — Tiwaz/Warrior

9. **ᚲ** — Kaunaz/Opening

10. **ᚹ** — Perth/Initiation

11. **ᛗ** — Mannaz/The Self

12. **X** — Gebo/Partnership

13. **ᛝ** — Ingwaz/Fertility

14. **Y** — Algiz/Protection

15. **ᚱ** — Raido/Journey

16. **ᚨ** — Anzus/Signals, Messages

17. **ᛟ** — Othila/Separation

18. **ᚢ** — Uraz/Strength

19. **M** — Ehwaz/Movement

20. **I** — Isa/Standstill

21. — The Blank Rune, Odin's Rune/ The Unknowable

22. **þ** — Thurisa/Gateway

23. **ᚹ** — Wanjo/Joy

24. **ᛃ** — Jera/Harvest

25. **ᛇ** — Eihwaz/Defense

What Is the Celtic Tree Calendar?

Based on the thirteen-month lunar calendar, each month was allocated a tree with special teachings, guides, totems, and deities. Each tree goes with a lunar cycle. There are fifteen trees represented, two of which share a month with another tree. Each tree is represented by an ogham letter, rune, and astrological sign. Special holidays fall into this scheme with the usual solar markings of the spring and fall equinoxes and the summer and winter solstices, as well as the cross-quarter lunar holidays that fall every six weeks between these solar dates. As with the Native American Medicine Wheel, the Wheel of the Year was and is followed in a similar fashion in native European paganism. This spirituality is essentially goddess-oriented and holds nature as sacred. We begin the year with the full moon nearest Samhain ("sow-in"), or October 31. This marks the ending of one year and the beginning of the Celtic New Year.

The Celts used this calendar as a time-keeping device and established names and special associations for their moons, developed over many years of ritual and experimentation. The Celtic tree system likely predates the druids, but they are usually given credit for creating this system. The trees the druids selected were sources of magic and myth in Celtic folklore; many of the trees were known to be attractive to the fairies and were also sources of herbs and medicines for the early Celts (McCoy, 68).

Druids are perhaps best known for worshipping in their sacred groves. It has been said that the name *druid* is based on the root word *dru,* meaning "immersed," combined with *uid*, "to know," meaning people with this title possessed great knowledge. Their sacred symbol was the serpent, which represented natural wisdom. They held their ceremonies in sacred groves and sought information from their tree oracles. Perhaps the most famous trees of the Celts were the yew and the oak. Yews are said to live for thousands of years and represent the soul's immortality. The Celts believed in reincarnation, communication with other planes of existence, and the afterlife. Celts revered

The Celtic Tree Calendar

1. Birch: Nov. 1–Nov. 28 / Beginnings / Snake, Phoenix, Eagle

2. Rowan: Nov. 29–Dec. 26 / Protection / Horse, Chiron

3. Alder: Dec. 27–Jan. 23 / Guidance/ Raven, Wren, Dragon

4. Willow: Jan. 24–Feb. 20 / Feminine Principle / Bee, Dove

5. Ash: Feb. 21–Mar. 20 / World Tree, As Above, So Below / Hanged Man, Dolphin

6. Hawthorn: Mar. 21–Apr. 17 / Cleansing / Fairies, White Stag

7. Oak: Apr. 18–May 15 / Strength / Bull

8. Holly: May 16–June 12 / Justice, Bringing Opposites Together / Swan

9. Hazel: June 13–July 10 / Intuition, Wisdom, Higher Perspective / Scarab, Turtle, Crab, Salmon

10. Apple (shares the month with Hazel): Choices, Female Lineages / Gaia, the Goddess

11. Vine: July 11–Aug. 7 / Prophecy / Lion

12. Ivy: Aug. 8–Sept. 4 / Labyrinth into Inner Knowing / Spider, Wolf

13. Reed: Sept. 5–Oct. 2 / Direct Action, Becoming a Hollow Reed / Owl, Pike

14. Blackthorn (shares the month with Reed): Negation / the Crone

15. Elder: Oct. 3–Oct. 30 / Renewal / Cranes, Storks, Ibis

The Day, Oct. 31: This was the most important day of the year, given extra attention in the Celtic cosmology. Recommitment to One's Spiritual Path; Death and Rebirth; Communication with Ancestors; Reconnection to One's Personal Guides and Guardians their ancestors and loved ones who had passed on, so to them, Oak represented the keeper of the greatest knowledge and wisdom, as well as one's ancestral memory.

The trees of the calendar were divided into three classes: chieftains, peasants, and shrubs. The division had nothing to do with their structure or size but with their level of importance within Celtic cosmology. Each tree was believed to be inhabited by spirits or dryads who were willing to share their healing powers with us (Conway, 154). Each tree also represented a portal into the unseen realm in which totems, guides, and deities could be reached for instruction and healing. The trees represented important principles of nature that would help humans to be good protectors and stewards of the land the Celts considered sacred.

Also included in appendix A are the Silver Fir, Gorse or Furze, Heather, White Poplar or Aspen, Yew, the Grove, Spindle, Honeysuckle, Beech, and the Sea. These have less to do with the months and more to do with particular times of the year and certain important elements. The additional trees also fill out the alphabet, providing vowels, vowel combinations, and some consonant combinations.

Why Follow the Moon Calendar Instead of the Sun Calendar?

There is controversy over when to begin the Celtic tree calendar. Many place the Birch month within the solar new year, in January. Others begin the Birch month at the beginning of November. The date of Samhain (October 31) was the ending of the old Celtic New Year and was traditionally observed as a descent into darkness for meditation and self-reflection. I have chosen November 1 as the beginning of this calendar as a way of staying within the older tradition that honors the lunar calendar and the goddess.

It is believed that it was Robert Graves, known for his book *The White Goddess,* who assumed that the first month of the Celtic tree calendar was solar and fell in January. However, Graves was not as interested in exact sabbat placements as he was in honoring the Goddess as the muse for poetry.

Samhain begins the lunar calendar and was the primary winter ceremony in the British Isles, just as Beltane was the primary summer ceremony that falls opposite Samhain in the Wheel of the Year. *Bealtaine* ("b'yol-tinna," meaning "May") was anglicized to Beltane (or Beltain). This springtime celebration falls in the Oak month of this system, which corresponds to the astrological sign Taurus and the month of May. Beltane and Taurus are opposite Scorpio and its month, November. In the Samhain-as-first-month-of-the-year system, placing the beginning of the year here flows with the arrangement of the Birch, Rowan, Alder, Willow, and Ash sequence rather than the Birch, Rowan, Ash, Alder, and Willow sequence of the solar calendar, in which the Oak month is in June.

Further, Alder is inseparable from the mythological Bran (the Celtic equivalent to Saturn or Kronos), who presides over Capricorn, January, and the third month of the lunar Samhain system. There is also no debate that the sequence of letters, trees, and months is accurate in this Samhain system, as identified by the placements of the letters on the joints of each finger. Refer to the hand diagram on page 20 to see these placements.

The troublesome fact is that there is a historical habit of referring to the Ogham alphabet as Beith (Birch), Luis (Rowan), and Nion (Ash)…in spite of the fact that we are using the order of Birch, Rowan, and Alder. The incorrect reference could be an abbreviation for the alphabet and is reinforced by the fact that the gesture of "the horned god" (used as a greeting or recognition of initiates) uses only the thumb, forefingers, and little fingers, which spells out Beith, Luis, and Nion. It is plausible that these three had been used as shorthand or as a nickname for the druidic mysteries and teachings rather than a description of the order of the trees as they fall within the calendar.

I find it most useful to consistently use sundown on October 31 as the beginning of the Celtic New Year. It neatly marks the end of the cycle of the thirteen moons (using the lunar calendar), and feels more connected to this ancient system of keeping time. I prefer the feeling of the year beginning with the harvest or summer's fruits, and the darkening after the equinox. It seems appropriate to me that we begin in the dark, honor the mysteries, and develop a new year out of the germinating seed of consciousness we intentionally plant, nurture, and cultivate.

ΤHE GiVEAWAY

Giving Back to the Trees

Gratitude is always your entrance fee and attention is your payment into the realm of the unseen. Spending some time in the presence of any tree, or calling upon a tree in meditation, is the giving of a gift and keeps the path of communication open, encouraging the dialogue between the seen and the unseen realms. If the spiritual dimensions are not recognized or contacted, the doors and portals eventually close. Thus, this practice becomes a sacred responsibility.

The next time you pass a tree, notice it, thank it, and send it your love and gratitude. You may notice that it requires something from you. Perhaps you need to touch it, water it, or pick up broken branches around its base—trees do respond to this. Perform your ceremonies outside under the cover of your own trees, or go to parks where there are larger groves. Being near them creates harmony in your environments and is especially healing for them.

Look in your own yard or property and see if a tree is diseased or not looking healthy. Be willing to bring in a natural arborist for advice on what your tree may need. Contact your local tree-disease specialist if you suspect that your tree is terminally afflicted. In times of drought or after wind and ice storms, it is especially important to consult an arborist or find information on how to properly water or take dead and broken branches from a tree. It is important to care for any new sapling, and you can find many different kinds of slow-release watering systems, especially useful in times of drought. Many trees are harmed by herbicides used in the lawn and garden, so be careful with this. Trees already stressed by drought can be killed in a heavy application of herbicide in the root zone, so avoid soil-activated herbicides around your tree.

When gathering bark, berries, branches, flowers, and leaves, wait until these fall naturally or watch for times when people prune or cut back their trees, and ask them if you can take some samples. Always ask the tree itself and give it your gratitude.

You may contact your local arborist for pruning advice, consult the Internet, or visit a library to find technical advice on how and where to make your cuts. It is important to prune your trees to ensure their health and your safety. It is necessary to prune diseased or insect-infested wood, thin the crown to increase airflow and reduce pest problems, and remove crossing and rubbing branches that interfere with the branches' ability to produce the food they need to sustain themselves. If left untreated, these branches die and are eventually shed. Pruning can be used to encourage trees to develop a strong structure and reduce the likelihood of damage during severe weather. Dead branches can be removed any time of the year but it is best to prune your trees during the dormant season, usually the late fall and winter.

Tools used should be sharpened, cleaned, and sanitized because they can contaminate the tree with fungi, bacteria, viruses, and other disease-causing microorganisms. Fresh wounds, e.g., where a tree branch has been severed, are perfect places for infections to begin so before each branch is cut, spray your tool with liquid household bleach diluted to 1 part to 9 parts water and clean the tools with soap and water after each use (bleach is corrosive to metal surfaces).

Be aware of projects like the Tree Corps, an offshoot (forgive the pun) of the Garden Project, which since 1994 has employed ex-convicts to plant and care for almost 10,000 trees throughout the San Francisco

Bay area, or the Green Belt Movement, begun by a Kenyan woman named Wangari, which now boasts thousands of registered groups in Kenya who have developed their own tree nurseries. Active members in this movement plant trees in an attempt to stave off encroaching desertification. The Green Belt Movement's work has fostered financial independence for many women, and has added to their political power and community voice.

Buy recycled toilet and facial tissue paper, and look for other recycled paper products that do not rely on the cutting of more trees. Mindfully attempting to live more simply can help the entire planet by using less water and energy. Make a commitment to consume wisely. Use your car less; walk more and ride your bike. Take your own cloth bags when grocery shopping rather than using paper or plastic. In colder months, turn your thermostat down and wear more layers. Help in local work parties to clean up and care for community parks and grounds that have trees. Begin to think of trees in your own local environment and what their particular needs may be. As I've hopefully shown here, there is no end to the projects that could be started.

Give your money and time to organizations that protect and plant trees. Donating to protect our national parks and natural open spaces in turn protects our forests. Get involved with projects that fight to preserve the planet's rainforests and threatened habitats. Also check out the Arbor Day Foundation.

Plant trees! There are numerous organizations with a presence on the Internet that will plant trees on your behalf. Simply go online and ask how you can help at organized events or how to plant a tree by yourself. While many sites accept donations, several are free or let you choose how to donate.

There are several ways you can become involved and help ecological efforts, but the most important thing you can do is to honor and give your gratitude to the trees that provide you with your oxygen and help provide you with clean air and water. Without the trees, we could not live, and they need us to be their stewards; we depend upon each other. I hope you will find some of these ideas useful in your own personal give-away to the trees. Be willing to take one tree-friendly action per month or even per year—it would be wonderful! Please refer to the Resources section in the back of this book for a list of some organizations to get you started.

THE CELTIC TREE CALENDAR

The First Fifteen of the Ogham Letters

Birch

BEITH–BIRCH

November 1–28
1st Lunation, November

Description: This tree has a tall, slender trunk that is often white or silver with papery bark that peels. They grow tall and have sparse foliage that blows in the wind and seems to whisper. The branches are long and graceful and the twigs are pliable. The leaves are small, heart-shaped, and come to a pointed end.

Ogham: Beth, Beith ("beh"), B: ⊢
Beginnings, endings, and a new start; cleansing; overcoming difficulties; pliability; re-establishing boundaries; purification and renewal; releasing old patterns and shedding unhelpful influences; resolution of conflict

Class: Peasant

Holiday: Nov. 1, the Celtic New Year, *Nos Galan Gof*

Rune: Berkano or Berkana ⟦ᛒ⟧
Growth, fertility rites, rebirth, new life, gestation and nourishment, the seed in the earth promising new life in the spring

Totems: Snake, Phoenix, Eagle

Astrology: Scorpio, October 22–November 21, ♏
"I create," a fixed water sign of feminine polarity
Symbols: scorpion, eagle, and/or phoenix

Ruling Planets: Mars ♂ and Pluto ♇, the 8th house of the chart

Body Parts: Rules the reproductive system

Colors: deep reds

Keywords: resourceful, secretive, passionate, intense, transforma-
    tion, elimination, reproduction, sexuality, power, the under-
    world, investigation, psychology, death, resurrection

The Beith/Birch Month

The Birch month begins with the Celtic New Year, the end and the
beginning time. This corresponds with the Day of the Dead in Mexican culture and is the day after our American Halloween, called All
Souls' Day in the Catholic tradition. It is a month of inceptions and
beginnings and this lunation is known as the Snow Moon. It offers
protection for children and represents purification, creativity, and
change. The color for the Birch month is white.

Birch brings the elements of purity and innocence coupled with the
awesome wisdom of the ancients. Look to your own lineage for wisdom. Receive the messages that come to you. Look at situations with
the eyes of a child and you will know how to enter heaven. Heaven
is right here in this place at this moment, depending upon how you
choose to see. Drop your need to judge, compartmentalize, or ana-
lyze. Allow each situation to teach you what is needed. Take the opportunity to look at this New Year with these new eyes. Birch offers
an opportunity to lay down misconceptions and judgments. We can
become receptive and open, as children are.

Childlike innocence can be augmented with ancient memory and
the wisdom of our ancestors. Birch offers us a doorway into our own
strong, innate inner knowing. Birch encourages us to follow our own
personal truth as seekers. It is a time to embrace spiritual resolve and
intention.

Birch offers a new start, but before the beginning can unfold, there
is work to do. What is unhelpful, outworn, outdated, or inhibiting

must be gathered and let go. Use Birch's branches to drive out energies you no longer desire in your space. The elimination process is aided by Scorpio's depth and vision. This sign's ruling planet, Pluto, calls for release of what no longer serves. Transformation and regeneration is offered. Herein lies death, but the promise is rebirth.

Birch also asks us for determination in overcoming difficulties. Let no distractions impede your progress once you begin. Like the white, slender Birch trunks that reach up and out of the entangled forest floor, you too can keep reaching for the light with determination and faith.

Birch also offers reconciliation, healing, peace, and resolution in times of conflict. Her branches are pliant and supple. Take a branch with you when you must resolve a conflict. She brings in the power of reconciliation.

Her slender white trunks earned her the name of the "Lady of the Woods." She reminds us of the snake who sheds her skin. Birch is always willing to let go of that which no longer serves. Be willing to let go of beliefs and habits that limit you. Ritualize this example every year. Let go of judgments and ways of seeing that stand in your way of joy and movement. We too can become like the beautiful, graceful Birch. Stand tall, and like her, reach toward the light in all you do.

Totems, Guides, and Deities

The totems of Birch are the snake, phoenix, and eagle; these coincide with Scorpio's energy. Scorpio's symbol, ♏, looks like an uncoiling snake, which stands for one's ability to go to great emotional depths and delve into the subconscious realms seeking revelation. The snake is a symbol of inner knowing and the intuitive arts and also represents kundalini energy (related to the root chakra) that rises in the spinal column, available for healing work. The priestesses of the Healing Temple of Hygeia, the goddess of health, used this energy for healing in ancient Greece, and we can too. Snakes remind us of our ability to heal and our ability to know. We are encouraged to share our seeing, hearing, speaking, and writing for healing.

Scorpio is ruled by Mars ♂ and Pluto ♇, and governs the reproductive system and the elimination system. Mars is the god of war, and Pluto is the god of death and resurrection. One of Scorpio's lessons is that by holding on and in too long, we harm ourselves. Letting go is the only path to healing. True power comes through faith, trust, and love; not control, manipulation, or fear. Death is part of life, and is to be honored and appreciated. As we approach winter, we enter Pluto's realm: the underworld. Although it is barren above, the seed is below, readying itself for new life.

The mythic phoenix rises from the ashes. We all know any journey into the depths can be painful, and yet if we are willing to look into the darkness and bring a lantern of light (truthful vision), we are better for the journey—there are valuable riches hidden in these depths. Magically, the phoenix rises, and in its flight, life begins anew. We have allowed the realm of magic to touch us. We are born again.

The eagle helps us see from a higher and more spiritual perspective, bringing about revelations and realizations. An eagle's ability to fly and soar high above allows for a breathtaking perspective, one we can use for insight. Elementally speaking, air energy can bring spaciousness into our emotions, as intellect can create balance and objectivity. The eagle brings a message of divinity to our daily lives to offer hope and inspiration. We aspire to our higher selves and rise above the need to seek revenge when threatened or hurt. We seek to rise above the need to strike out of insecurity, or perceived threat, like the scorpion.

In this month is a portal of the Crone. There are many goddesses who represent the crone energy of death and rebirth. In Egypt, Hathor is the life giver, and Isis used her regenerative energy to re-animate Osiris after his murder. Neith, Nepthys, and Sekhmet are powerful Egyptian guardians between life and death. Mother Mut, the vulture, is the oldest of the Egyptian wisdom keepers. Spider

Woman is the mother of life to the Native Americans. Tiamet of ancient Babylon is the dragon mother who protects and wields death.

The Sidhe, pronounced "shee," or fairy folk, are also interested in these regenerative cycles. The Sybil, as the oracle of Delphi, offers us her ancient sight. Cerridwen, Hecate, Baba Yaga, the Gaelic banshee, and Cailleach the hag all carry the crone energy of death and rebirth.

At this time of year when the dark comes early and the days are short, we honor and respect our connection with what has gone before. We can feel the thinness of the veil that separates the worlds. Honor these crones well and they will shed their protection over you. Give gratitude to your own grandmothers and great-grandmothers in your ancestral lineages. Do not fear their lessons and teachings, for in the end is always the beginning. Do not fear aging and death; the crones teach that death is but a doorway to another world of consciousness and that there is in fact no death, and no end.

Do not fear going within and being quiet. The pace of our busy lives often prevents us from slowing down and getting in touch with our inner world and soul center. If you make time, the crones will bless you.

Guided Meditation

Imagine you find yourself climbing a rocky hill somewhere in the British Isles. It is a November night and the sky is cold, clear, and dark. You are wrapped warmly in your own cloak, and your hood is cinched up around your head. The stars are shining brightly, and the moon is full and illuminates the landscape below. Notice how free and exhilarated you feel. You climb to a plateau, and just ahead, you see a grove of tall silver birch trees, gracefully dancing in the wind. You can hear the leaves singing to you. You can see the slender trunks of the trees gleaming in the moonlight. Within the grove you are approaching, you know the priestess awaits you.

As you enter the grove, you see a circle of lit torches and many priestesses standing in a large circle beckoning you forward; they make room for you to enter. At the center of the circle you approach a beautiful crone. Take notice of her clothing and her facial features—is she kind? Severe? Wise? She has been waiting for you for a long time and greets you with love and compassion.

This is the Priestess of Birch. She knows how to connect you to ancient memory and the wisdom of the ancestors down through time. She beckons you to come closer and stand in front of her. She takes your hands in hers and smiles at you with acceptance and recognition. She speaks: "Daughter, we welcome you. We have been waiting for you to return for a long, long time. We acknowledge you as the seer, knower, and healer that you are. Your many gifts will be shown tonight. We acknowledge your own inner truth and loving nature. You have the Tree of Life within you. It is your birthright and your own true nature. So be it."

In this moment, you shapeshift and magically find yourself morphing into a huge ancient tree. Take a moment to feel this experience... (pause) Notice the huge expanse of branches that reach for the sky; your large, steady, and strong trunk; and your mighty root system that extends down deep into Mother Earth... (pause)

Turn your attention now to your root structure and follow the roots down through the earth. Feel the rootedness and strength of this, your lower self. See all the roots as they travel down and receive nourishment from mother Gaia. Here in your lower self is where you keep your memories; here are all stories of the past. In this place, everything is recorded and filed, though you may not be conscious of it. Your root system contains your elemental self—the power and the ability to change air, water, and food into energy. Here lies the special power that keeps your body healthy. This is the part of you that serves you well, and manifests your dreams and desires. Always talk to your lower self with love and appreciation.

Doubts, guilt, fears, hurts, and beliefs that no longer serve you are stored here as well. These roots must be gently cleaned and cleared of these blockages so nutrients can make it all the way up into your middle and Higher Self. It is hard for your lower self to talk to your Higher Self when it is feeling low or unworthy; it can't send its prayers. That is why we are giving special love and recognition to your lower self today. We send a gentle trickle of water to clear and cleanse these roots of any negativity and clear any clusters of distress. Let them go into the earth for further transformation. Take a moment to really feel this cleansing...

Next, focus your attention on the trunk of your tree. This is your middle self. Here is the structure of your conscious life and your everyday contact with your social world. You think, feel, and make decisions here; it is here your right and left brain communicate with each other. Your trunk represents your unique physical body and personality through which you express yourself upon the Earth in this life. Notice your bark, stance, and sturdiness; this is made up of thoughts and beliefs, feelings, and behaviors. Consider your trunk to be like the "boss" of the tree; it connects heaven and earth. Your trunk is your intentions and decisions; your will and purpose. Know that you can have more connection with all parts of yourself through intention made by this middle self. With your intention, send love to your lower self—it does so much for you and looks up to you. Give gratitude to your Higher Self for its unconditional love and higher wisdom. Remember that not every thought or feeling is worth giving attention to. Feed only those thoughts, feelings, and actions that make your life beautiful. Take a moment to contemplate this...

Direct your attention to the limbs, branches, and leaves of your tree. Follow all the way out as you stretch up into your boughs and leaves that touch the sky. This is your Higher Self, reaching upwards to higher and higher dimensions. It is in this place you receive unconditional love and acceptance from higher beings, and from the universal consciousness of oneness and unity called Spirit. You need this spiritual nourishment in the same way the trees need sunlight to make food. Here is where your spiritual "mana" resides. Take a moment to feel this part of you and to give your gratitude to this wise place...

Now it is time to step out of your tree and reclaim your physical body again. From your human perspective, take a moment to view your tree. Look at its lower, middle, and higher parts. Notice how all three parts of this tree work together in harmony and support each other. All three are necessary and important; no part is "better" than another. Remember that this arrangement is also a reflection of your physical composition. Set the intention that you will begin to know how to bring harmony to these parts of yourself so they can work together. Doing so is your first initiation into the trees' teachings.

You now become aware of the Priestess, who is watching you, smiling. She reminds you that the birch tree has many teachings. The birch is a tree that asks you to look at everything and everyone around you with wide-open, non-judging eyes; the Priestess calls these "eyes of true sight." Are you willing to avoid categorizing people's actions or any ongoing situation in your life as right or wrong, good or bad? The Priestess suggests you simply regard things as they happen without any preconception; in this way, you will be able to perceive wholeness.

The Priestess takes holy water from a crystal bowl and gives it to you, uttering a blessing as she touches your third eye: "As above, so below." Spirit of Higher Self—only love, compassion and understanding. Spirit of Middle Self—conscious mind, feeling, and action. Spirit of Lower Self—nature spirit creating and manifesting form. As the tree is, so are you. All in perfect form. Love yourself. Forgive yourself. Trust yourself, for you are precious beyond your understanding. Blessed are you this night, goddess or god that you are, and know that you are loved. Claim your birthright as healer, seer, and knower. See clearly in this moment your own special gifts (pause); are you willing to claim your birthright of love and light? And so through the portal of Birch, you walk into a new year of your life. You have passed through a new threshold and you begin your initiation into the healing power of the trees. So it is, blessed be!

Take a moment to give the Priestess your gratitude. Thank the universe for your own design—it is sacred. Give gratitude for the basic form you share with the tree: your lower, middle, and higher selves. Nod in gratitude to the many priestesses who support you here, and give your gratitude to the sacred and holy birch grove of new beginnings.

It is time to leave the birch trees and this special place. Leave the plateau and come back down the hill to your waking self, but know that you are transformed. Remember that this is a new beginning and that every moment is a new beginning. Shed the old ideas, beliefs, and judgments that separate you from others. Become innocent once more. Are you willing to let go of things you have been carrying that no longer serve a purpose? If you are, simply let the weight slip off your shoulders and onto the ground. And most important of all, ask yourself if you are ready to love yourself fully. As you walk through the month of November, make a commitment to treat yourself with love, respect, and kindness. Let go of any judgments and unkind words. No more recriminations and condemnations. Resolve to learn better how parts of yourself can work together in your best interest to create the life you desire. Become your own best friend first! Ground and breathe, and when you are ready, return to this room and to this time and space. Open your eyes. Choose to look through your open and loving heart. Record your journey in your journal.

Birch Healing

Invoke this tree's power to help you with endings. Birch will support you in releasing old patterns and shedding unhelpful or negative influences.

She will also help you reach towards the light for renewed hope when you are troubled or worried.

She can bring in clarity through confusion when you can't see the forest for the trees. She reminds you to look upwards and consider the bigger picture rather than focus on the problems and concerns at hand. She can bring in higher perspective.

In any kind of conflict, she can bring in the energy of resolution for the highest good of all concerned.

Birch reminds us that we shed our "skin" yearly just as she sheds her bark. Find a piece of her bark, but do not remove the bark entirely or the tree will die. You usually can find pieces around the tree. These can be soaked, pressed, and flattened. Write your intentions for the new year. Keep this on your altar to remind you of new beginnings.

You can gather branches you find around the tree and make a broom. Tie them and place a thick branch into the middle of the bundle. Sweep the area when you want to drive away especially negative intrusions of energy in your home or work area. Birch brings in purification and renewal, so use your broom when you are about to begin new projects.

Birch's branches can be used to redefine boundaries that have weakened or been threatened. Hold a branch and set your intention for the placement of new psychic boundaries, or draw actual physical boundaries as you walk over your property or around your home.

Bring in birch branches, leaves, flutes, and bark into your Celtic New Year's rituals and ceremonies to ensure a wonderful start and blessed new beginnings.

LUIS-ROWAN

November 29–December 26
2nd Lunation, December

Description: Rowan is a pretty tree that may have up to fifteen leaflets that form compound leaves. They have white flowers in late spring. The leaves are long and pointy. Red or orange clusters of berries that have little five-pointed stars or pentacles appear in autumn. The bark is dark gray and smooth.

Ogham: Luis ("loo-ish" or "l'weesh"), L: ⊨
Protection against enchantment or the control of others; astral travel; connection to ecstasy, universal unconditional love, and higher consciousness

Class: Peasant

Holidays: December 21 or 22, Winter Solstice, Alban Arthuan, Yule, Midwinter

Rune: Laguz ⎸↿⎸
Flow, water, sea, powers that nourish, a fertility source, awakening of the intuitive or lunar side of your nature, a time for cleansing, self-transformation, telepathy, wisdom, intention, communication with the collective unconscious, astral travel

Totems: Horse, Centaur, Chiron

Rowan

Astrology: Sagittarius, November 22–December 22, ♐
    "I perceive," a mutable masculine fire sign
    Symbol: the centaur
    Ruling Planet: Jupiter ♃, the 9th house of the chart
    Body Parts: Rules the hips, thighs, and flesh
    Colors: purple and deep blue
    Keywords: aspiring, exploring, freedom-loving, foresight

The Luis/Rowan Month

Within this month we celebrate the Winter Solstice, which occurs on December 21 or 22, marking the beginning of winter and the rebirth of the sun. Rowan enlists the help of Chiron the centaur and the energy of Sagittarius. Its colors are gray and red. This lunation is the Oak Moon: the spirit moon and the astral travel moon. It is the moon of visions, and encourages self-empowerment, healing, and divination. As a portal, this moon offers us an invitation to expand our vision and philosophy.

Rowan is also known at the European Mountain Ash, the Quickbeam, the Sorb Apple, and the Lady of the Mountain. This tree bears red or orange berries that have a little pentacle of dark color at their center. Rowan grows easily on the sides of mountains and can sprout in crevices and other unlikely places. This tree teaches us to not give up when obstacles block our growth; we must keep going in the face of adversity, and thrive in spite of a lack of nurturance or acknowledgement. Rowan represents the indomitable life force. Hanging rowan branches over our home's entrances strengthens our positive life energies and encourages our desire to use personal power for creating good things in the world. Rowan helps us withstand temptations and aids in releasing negativity.

Rowan is a tree of vision, healing, and psychic powers. It was a favorite tree of the druids, who referred to it as the "Witch tree," a label meant in the best sense of the word. Let's leave the popular cartoon world of the wicked queen/stepmother/witch archetype, and journey back into the times when the crone was honored for her wisdom. Let us honor the generations of wise women in all cultures around the world who have studied the healing properties of herbs, plants, and trees and shared them with their communities for healing. I am grateful they have passed the information for healing down through the ages despite the threats to their own lives and safety. It is my hope we can fully reclaim their knowledge and practices. Other names for this tree within this context include Wicken-tree, Wild Ash, Witchbane, Witchwood, and the Tree of Life.

The idea of astral travel, or "flying on broomsticks," is really the experience of ecstatic communion with the divine. When we experience breaking out of our mundane or purely physical existence, we can enter our spiritual body, which can travel anywhere and experience the bliss of union with all that is.

Ogham marks were usually carved on sticks of Rowan and were used for divination. Rowan increases your divination abilities, and helps to expand your view. When you feel stuck, ask Rowan for possibilities you may not have considered. It can aid in understanding the various outcomes of a situation. It is also helpful in focusing on the decision of whether progress in a situation is useful or if it is best to cease. Rowan provides protection, especially for the feminine principle. It is good for grounding, and can help you reconnect with universal love.

Rowan is also known for its protective qualities, and is sensitive to the power of enchantment. Sometimes we recognize our enemies and sometimes we don't. Rowan will protect you against seduction and anything that means to overpower you. She will inform you when you have failed to heed your own inner knowing, or if you have blinded yourself to red flags you may have seen, but ignored. She will wake you when you are in the thrall of harmful or vindictive powers and will help you regain control of your senses so you can distinguish bad from good, or harm from help. Rowan encourages using your spiritual strength to turn away from anything that threatens your serenity and purpose. Luis supports your controlling your own life.

Totems, Guides, and Deities

Rowan's main totem is the horse. The relationship between horses and humans has always been a powerful one, but it underlies a need for a respect of what is wild and an appreciation of what is wild in each of us. In shamanic use, horses could help humans "ride" to other realms of the spirit, bring back messages from deities, or retrieve forgotten wisdom. To enter a trance, shamans used the drum, whose beat simulated the drumming of hooves and the sensation of travel, or flight. This flying-motion type of trance brought visions, and shamans would return with teachings and messages for the rest of the tribe. The horse served (and still does serve) as a vehicle and guide to divine revelations, is related to astral travel, and serves as our magical companion. Whether we dream or travel while in trance, we extend beyond the usual boundaries and can fly anywhere.

Epona, the white mare, is the ancestral horse totem of much of Celtic Europe. She is the mare mother of the divine colt son of the Gaelic Celts. We see a common theme in the Welsh legends of Rhiannon, Modron, and Mabon: the horse shapeshifts to maiden, mother, and crone as appropriate, and bestows power and sovereignty on those who offer proper respect and homage. Epona travels between the worlds and is the author of the mysteries.

The mare is an ancestor of the Horse Clan and takes the position of the southeast in the ancient British wheel of totems. This direction is connected to the Pleiades. The Uffington White Horse in Oxfordshire, UK, is a huge representation that can only be seen in its entirety from the air. It is carved in the earth in white chalk and looks over the Vale of Pewsey. It is said that the ancestors of Britain were the seven daughters of Rhiannon and their home was the Pleiades. Perhaps this is a clear clue to our ancestry originating in the stars.

Another totem for this time of year is Chiron, the centaur from Greek mythology. Centaurs were a race of creatures that had the torso and head of a human and the body of a (sometimes winged) horse. They were depicted carrying bows and arrows, giving them raw archer energy. Chiron in particular is the archetype of the wounded healer—wise but crippled. He brings information to us through our body symptoms. It is often in illness and its discomfort that we seek out the meanings of our physical symptoms. It is also true that pain can be an important teacher. Here we are forced to stop and look at ourselves, and heal what is causing us pain. Chiron has much to share with us and teaches us to listen to our body's symptoms. He gives us knowledge of how to heal.

Chiron's bow and arrow provides us with a clue as to how we might use our mental abilities. Our minds are like powerful bows, and we can notch our arrows of thought and release them into manifestation, but it takes much practice and mastery. Sagittarius asks us to continually expand our beliefs and reach for higher consciousness. Once we understand that we create our reality with our thinking fueled by our emotional states, we can become co-creators with the universal life force. The power of belief and the choice of our thinking can affect our bodies and bring states of imbalance back into a state of perfection. Body symptoms can sometimes be related to problematic thinking and the limiting beliefs we hold out of fear. We can therefore correct things more easily when symptoms first appear. I'm not claiming to understand the causes of every disease, but I do know that we can affect our bodies through the conscious choice of positive thoughts, beliefs, and actions.

The name "rowan" comes from *runa*, a word which in ancient Norse means "magical charm" and means "magician" in Sanskrit. We enter the world of possibilities, of co-creation with spirit, and bring the power of miracles and healing to our world. There is no difference between dream time and the mundane world except in our own beliefs. Sagittarius challenges us to loosen limitations of our own belief systems and expand our consciousness to embrace all possibilities, including joy, enthusiasm, ecstasy, and healing.

Guided Meditation

Take an astral journey with Chiron, your spirit horse, and the Priestess of Rowan, playing any music that puts you in a dreamy space.

Ground and center, and breathe into your heart. Inhale, pulling energy from the earth up into your heart and exhale it out in all directions. Pull the energy from above through your crown chakra and into your heart, and breathe it out in all directions. Take a few moments to experiences this breath ...

In your mind, travel to a place in nature that you love. It is winter and you are dressed warmly. From the sky comes your spirit horse who invites you to climb upon her for an astral ride. Take a moment to greet your horse and take in her beauty and power. Chiron soon arrives and indicates he will accompany you on your journey. He has a handsome human upper body and the lower body of a beautiful, strong flying horse. You exchange greetings, and take off into the wintry clouds. Look down at the world from the sky. Notice the perspective. Take a moment to feel the freedom of flight and to let yourself soar ... (pause)

As you fly high above the earth, your spirit horse and Chiron eventually fly you to the dimension of the Priestess of Rowan. Looking down, you see a landscape filled with beautiful rowan trees, ripe with their clusters of red and orange berries. Your companions land you safely within a grove. Chiron places his hands upon your heart and sends you healing energy for any physical problem you may be having. Take a moment to receive any message he may have for you about a particular bodily trouble ... (pause) Give him your gratitude.

As you dismount, your attention turns towards the beautiful grove of rowan you're standing in. As you breathe in the wonderful forest scent, you find there is inspiration everywhere in this place of all possibilities. In the distance, you see a beautiful priestess approaching you. She has a radiant smile, and walks right up to you; she places a crown of rowan leaves and berries on your head. Look deeply into her eyes and see the love she has for you.

Tell her what you yearn for. Tell her what your dreams are. Tell her how you would like to bring light to the planet. In seeking her protection and guidance, she will become your staunch ally. Take some time to receive her offerings … (pause)

Show her places in your body, mind, or soul that are distressing you. She will gladly lighten your load, give you inspiration, renew your enthusiasm, and make you laugh. She will heal you. Feel the grand possibility of all miracles. Agree to enlarge your belief system to include more and more of the mystery and magic of creation as you connect to these higher dimensions of love … (pause)

Thank the priestess for her presence in the world. When you feel ready, fly home with Chiron and your spirit horse; they will bring you safely back to this dimension. Take a moment to say goodbye to Chiron and your spirit horse. Give them your gratitude. Know that they are your allies now, and are at your service. Your spirit horse is ready to fly with you whenever you call. Chiron is ready to help you understand any physical ailments and to assist your healing.

Ground and center in this place and in this time. Stay here quietly for a moment and ponder the beauty of your experience. Upon returning, write your experiences in your journal. Do this to ground yourself, because, like dreams, details are easy to forget if you wait too long to record them.

Rowan Healing

Use your divination tools to seek guidance and counsel. The tarot, I Ching, astrology, runes, ogham, and other methods give you a direct line to other realms that encourage your growth and your happiness. Try the Celtic oracle known as scrying. Use a crystal ball or even a bowl of water to gaze into. Soften your vision and allow the images to appear.

Rowan offers you protection from those you do not trust, or from those who have the power to confuse and manipulate you. She will help you see through any false glamour interfering with your common sense and judgment. She is especially helpful in strengthening your intuition before finalizing business deals or venturing further in a relationship with someone new. She will also help determine if it is best to go further with new friendships or new plans.

Rowan connects you to ecstasy and enjoying the use of your senses. Read poetry, paint a picture, listen to music, sing, or gather together in ritual. Take time to be quiet and take another astral journey with your spirit horse.

Ask Chiron to help you understand your body symptoms, because once they have your attention, they often dissipate. Symptoms carry a message from your soul, and remember that the correct answer is oftentimes the most obvious or simple one.

When things go wrong for me or I experience physical discomfort, I reflect on the kinds of thoughts I'm having. Rowan reminds me to rework or dispose of thoughts that are harmful, limiting, and disheartening. I am reminded to "clean up" my thoughts and feelings. If I can return to at least a neutral state, things seem to change and improve. There might be some personal work I have to perform involving forgiveness or putting things right. This personal work is a bit like taking out the garbage on a daily or weekly basis—it's common-sense maintenance. In moments when I doubt my personal power, the centaur reminds me that I am responsible for what I create—and that I am a powerful creator.

Alder

FEARN–ALDER

December 27–January 23
3rd Lunation, January

Description: Alders are often the first trees to grow in a forest after a fire or some other form of devastation; they are often found close to water. These trees have wide and rounded leaves that come to a point, with feathered edges and many lines drawn out to the edges from the central vein of the leaf. The trunks are slender and they grow fairly tall. Alders have catkins (tassels) and little cones they drop for reproduction.

Ogham: Fearn ("fair-un"), F and V: ⊨
Guidance; oracular; prophecy; helps when making choices; spiritual protection, especially in disputes; stability; strong foundations

Class: Chieftain

Holiday: Celtic solar new year, January 1

Rune: Fehu 〔ᚠ〕
Possessions and wealth as well as reputation and personal power, fulfillment, ambition, rewards, nourishment, share your blessings

Totems: Birds—wrens, ravens, crows, kingfishers;
Dragon, Bran and Branwen

Astrology: Capricorn, December 21–January 19, ♑︎

"I Use," a cardinal earth sign of feminine polarity

Symbol: the mountain goat with a dolphin's tail

Ruling Planet: Saturn ♄, the 10th house in the chart

Body Parts: Rules the bones, skin, knees

Colors: dark shades

Keywords: practical, dependable, hard working, responsible, conscientious, prudent, reliable, efficient, ambitious, authority, leadership, reputation

The Fearn/Alder Month

The Alder month marks the beginning of the Celtic solar year. Nobility, strength, and great competency are seen in the alder; it is said to represent deep winter. This month is aligned with Capricorn's energies. Capricorn is a cardinal or initiating earth sign that loves authority, leadership, power, and reputation. It usually receives recognition because it is willing to take on responsibility and leadership. It is related to career, worldly honor, and prestige. It is the third month in the tree calendar, and the number three is representative of the Goddess as maiden, mother, and crone. Numerologically, three is the number of creativity and of Mother Earth. Fearn holds both male and female powers, and is good for balance. Its color is crimson. This lunation is called the Wolf Moon.

In deep winter, we like to come indoors and get all cozy and comfy. It is a time to go within, to sleep and dream, to read, write, and rest. We end one solar year and begin another. We make our New Year's resolutions and evaluate the old as we welcome in the new. We long to bring light into the darkness and get much enjoyment out of candles and fireplaces. We celebrate with festivities of light and bring our family and friends together. Alder supports both inner musings and outward celebrations.

Alder is associated with water, emotion, and feelings and represents support and foundations. It seems natural, then, that bridges in old Europe were often made of alder. Water spirits called undines love this tree, as does the magical unicorn. Undines help clear and cleanse, as well as protect, all the water on the planet. Alder offers spiritual protection, so if you are in a dispute of any kind, invoke the dryad of alder and this tree's spirit will act as a "bridge over troubled waters."

The alder possesses a strong male energy that will offer you backbone and strength in a fight. Alder has a strong fighting ability and was a powerful fighter in the Welsh poem *Cad Goddeu*, or "The Battle of the Trees," in which it was honored with the name "the Battle Witch of the Wood." Ancient Celts used alderwood to create hot fire for their metalworking.

Alder also contains female aspects—consider the tree's affinity for water, a feminine element. Alder's dual nature can be used to balance male and female attributes, and can substitute whatever attribute you need in any situation. When cut, alder turns a rich red color that appears much like bleeding, representing the feminine shedding of blood. This tree also has a sacrificial quality in that it is the first to grow in a new forest, or a recovering one. Alder roots encourage nitrogen replacement in soil, allowing other trees to grow above and beyond her—the "mothering" quality of self-sacrifice for the growth and goodness of one's children. Alder also sets its buds in a spiral, a powerful feminine symbol of the continuation of life.

Totems, Guides, and Deities

Druids often used birds to make their divinations. The kingfisher, wren, and raven are all totems of Alder. Wren was studied for messages and warnings concerning health and well-being. Raven was considered a master of prophecy and traveler between worlds, and was associated with the Welsh story of Bran (see below). The beginning of a new solar year was an important time for consulting an oracle. Ask Raven to bring you insight as you do astrology, or read the tarot, crystal bowl, tea leaves, or scry in the waters of a cauldron.

Raven, crow, and blackbird are all powerful helpers this month. They are alert and intelligent and have a knowing, mysterious air about them. In fact, they represent the mysteries and occult in many cultures. In legends, they can travel between worlds, carry messages, and also serve as harbingers and portents.

Bran and Branwen were said to be able to traverse different worlds, and were considered the ancestral siblings of old Britain. They were to the Welsh what Isis and Osiris were to ancient Egyptians. They are associated with oracular power along with their totems: the raven and the wren. Branwen sent a magical wren to Bran to rescue her from Ireland. Her message to Bran was that she was not being treated kindly by her husband, the Irish King.

Bran the Blessed led his warriors on a rescue mission. He spanned an impassable waterway with his gigantic body and formed a bridge for his army to cross into Ireland. Although he was mortally wounded in his return from Ireland after saving his sister, his head was carried back to Britain where its oracular power was well known. Bran's head was said to have been finally buried in London with a pronouncement that it should not be dug up, as its burial protected the kingdom. Ages later, Arthur dug it up and sure enough, the Saxons invaded. Bran and the raven are renowned for their ability to see into the future. To this day, Bran is associated with the ravens at the Tower of London. The ravens' stay at the Tower is said to ensure the realm's protection.

The astrological sign of Capricorn also applies to the alder month. The symbol for Capricorn, ♑, is the horned sea beast or water dragon. The half-goat/half-fish figure shows the ascension from the depths to the heights. It also infers the mother principle of the waters as connecting with the father principles of sky and spirit. The merging of two different creatures represents the quest for balance between above and below, outer and inner, and male and female.

Another important totem of the Fearn/Alder month is Dragon, a divine animal ancestor of the Welsh. The great wizard Merlin is said to have been fathered by a dragon. Dragon signifies ancient genetic memory and the protection of ancient wisdom. These creatures will help you keep in touch with your ancestral heritage. The[y] guardians and will protect you and your valuables. The[y] you connect with the ability to be earthly, stable, and materialistically secure. Dragons are the guardians of our well-being and of our inner treasures as well.

Guided Meditation

Note: you may want to record this journey ahead of time and add meditation music so you can fully experience this journey. Take a moment to reflect on your own ancestry. Gather in your mind the various places in the world you know your ancestors are from. Think about these places and give gratitude for their being part of your ancestry. Think about family members who have passed on, and stories about various people in your family. Also be mindful of places around the world you are drawn to and the various spiritual lineages that manifest from those places. These places mark your subconscious origins and are part of today's meditation as well. Now, take a moment to think of a question you have not been able to find an answer for. When ready, close your eyes, and ground and center yourself.

Travel in your mind's eye to a grove of alder trees. The trees sway with the wind and offer you welcome. Know that alder is especially helpful in guidance, prophecy, or protection. As you arrive, be willing to feel the protection all around you; alder is here to ensure your safety. Allow its strength to encircle you. Respond to the trees; let them know what you especially need strength and protection for in your life … (pause)

Loved ones from your ancestry slowly appear and move towards you. They draw near but are respectful of your personal space. Some you recognize and some you don't. Some are dressed in clothing from the times they lived in, and some are dressed in clothing based on their ethnicities. Some are not from your family but represent the spiritual lineages around the world that you feel drawn to. There may be a Native American medicine woman, an Australian aborigine, a Tibetan master, or an Indian guru ... Notice their great love and appreciation of you. Though these people may have spoken a different language than you in their lifetimes, you can freely converse with them in this space. Feel their encouragement and listen for any messages they might have ... (pause) These people represent your spiritual support team.

Next, you notice birds flying closely and chirping and chattering around you. Out of the flock, one raven lands, and hops and skips close to you. You notice a gleam in his eye while he cocks his head as if examining you. He has an answer for your question—he is the oracle. He is willing to be consulted in your quest for guidance. Be willing to ask your question and receive your answer ... (long pause) When finished with his message, he flies to the shoulder of a beautiful priestess approaching from the distance.

The Priestess of Alder wears a soft, green full-length cloak, and around her neck is a pendant boasting a picture of a dragon. Her eyes are green and her red hair is long and flowing, blowing gently off of her shoulders in the wind. She asks you to tell her what your favorite oracle is. Take a moment to contemplate this: is it the runes, the tarot, astrology, the I Ching, the tree cards, the ogham, or any others not mentioned here? After you tell her, she places a hand on your third eye and blesses you in her own ancient language. You feel the transmission. She finishes by asking only one thing of you: to spend some time with your favorite oracle or to see someone who can read for you that you trust. Through your chosen oracle, she will come to speak with you and share her wisdom.

It is time to give gratitude to the alder grove for its protection. Give gratitude to the priestess, your ancestors, the birds, and especially your own oracular raven. The priestess takes your hand and holds it to her heart and you feel her love. Your ancestors joyfully clap their hands and yell together in one big "hurrah" to celebrate your life and to encourage you forward. Again give your heart-filled gratitude. It is wonderful to know you are never really alone and that you have an entire lineage of support behind you in everything you do, at all times.

When you are ready, return to this time and place. Ground and center, and after a few moments, open your eyes. It is always a good idea to write your journey down afterwards to help ground it and keep it fresh in your memory.

Scrying

Scrying is a uniquely Celtic art. It serves as a beginning place for inward journeys, using the imagination. Scrying requires us to see at a distance, but with inner sight. This seeing does not use our eyes in the conventional sense; it requires seeing with imagination. When you are seeking guidance about a certain issue, you can look into a vessel of water and allow your imagination to provide you with information—usually in vague images. You can also scry within your mind by imagining a megalithic standing stone and allowing images to form upon the stone in your mind's eye.

You can use almost any type of vessel for scrying. I use a pretty, opaque blue glass bowl or sometimes a small cauldron. A white china dish is also suitable; and it's said that copper bowls give a special vibration when used for scrying.

It is a good idea to dedicate any scrying vessel you use, and use it only for that purpose. Fill the bowl with clear water, focusing your intention, and ask that both water and vessel reveal the magical information you require. As mentioned earlier, you can un-focus your eyes and "look" at nothing, or you can concentrate on your question while gazing at the water, and close your eyes afterwards to receive the answers you need. Answers can take many forms; you might see objects, letters or words, you might feel sensations or hear sounds or speech, or a sudden thought may pop into your head.

Often, otherworldly beings will show up, that know things that you don't and are willing to share with you. Treat them with respect. When beings show up that belong to the class of powerful spirits like angels, intelligences from higher dimensions, deities, or devas, they may test you before giving away their secrets. If you earn their respect, they will share their magical teachings.

Alder Healing

When you seek balance, call on Alder, keeping in mind its dualistic nature: a water-loving female tree, but also a masculine tree connected to fighting for a position or standing your ground.

Collect alder branches, twigs, berries, and leaves and place them on your altar when you use any oracular tool.

Invite the birds as allies. Watch for messages from the birds around you. Treat ravens and crows kindly, for they are very intelligent and have long memories.

Buds of the alder are set in spirals, powerful symbols of everlasting life and resurrection. When you feel a need for regeneration, collect some buds and invite renewal into your life.

Alder leaves can be made into a poultice to reduce swellings. Mash up some of the leaves, moisten with warm milk, and tie them over the tissue that needs treatment.

When you are out in nature or on a long hike, you can place alder leaves inside your boots or shoes, as they are cooling and soothing.

Alder can also be used to make wonderful dyes. The flower makes a strong green dye, the bark can be used to make a red dye, and a brown dye comes from the twig. All these garment colors are associated with the clothes of the fairies and elves and thus the alder was known as the Elf King.

Alder wood is oily and water-resistant and is therefore good for building bridges and any other outdoor object. The wood also lends itself quite well to wood-working; it can be made into toys, brooms, and even shoes or clogs.

Alder is not a suitable firewood source; fires built from it don't burn well. One of its wonderful attributes is that it can be planted to enrich otherwise poor quality soil because it replaces nitrogen in the soil, allowing others trees and plants to grow. It is also useful to prevent soil erosion.

When you feel lonely, remember the circle of ancestors that came to you in your guided meditation. Imagine them standing around you and listen for their messages. They will remind you that you are loved and that you are never alone.

Sometimes we cannot see the forest for the trees. If you are confused and unclear, seek out the oracle—the priestess of Alder will inform you. Seek guidance outside yourself. Ask others for help when you feel too isolated or stuck. In reaching out, the people you meet can be quite amazing. In my struggle to understand my spiritual journey, I met many wonderful healers and helpers. I also found the books and tools I needed. The people I met helped me heal myself and change. There are many talented healers and wonderful methods and tools available these days—enlarge your cauldron of helpers.

Willow

SAILLE—WILLOW

January 24—February 20
4th Lunation, February

Description: These trees are often found near water. They help stabilize banks of rivers, streams, and lakes. The can grow quite large but there are also shrublike varieties. Willow braches are long, slender, and flexible, with long, tapered leaves that have serrated margins. They form catkins (tassels) in early spring. There are more than a hundred kinds of willows. The most popular and recognizeable are the weeping and corkscrew varieties. The trunks are usually thick and rough with irregular ridges.

Ogham: Saille ("sahl'yeh," "SAHL-yuh"), S: ᚄ
The feminine principle; cooperation; fertility; the moon; mother, daughter, and crone; community interest; shared power

Class: Peasant

Holiday: February 2, Candlemas, Imbolc

Rune: Sowelo ᛋ
Feminine perspective, wholeness, feminine power, moonlight, cooperation and organization, peace and harmony of the collective, receptivity, and the reflected light of the sun

Totems: Bee, Dove, the Goddess (the maiden aspect), Brigit

Astrology: Aquarius, January 19 or 20—February 18 or 19, ♒

"I know," a fixed masculine air sign

Symbol: the water (energy) bearer

Ruling Planets: Saturn ♄ and Uranus ♅, the 11th house of the chart

Body Parts: Rules the circulation and the ankles

Colors: iridescent blues

Keywords: communicative, inventive, altruistic, detached, original, innovative, higher realms of consciousness, spiritual nourishment and wisdom, reform, rebellious, group oriented

The Saille/Willow Month

The Willow month includes the cross-quarter holiday of Candlemas or Imbolc, falling on February 2. This is the festival for Brigit or Brighid (there are many spellings of her name). In more modern times, February 2 is Groundhog Day, when we find out whether we have six more weeks until spring. This is the goddess Brigit's domain: the time when the seeds begin to quicken deep within the earth, represented by the crescent moon. Of the triple aspects of the goddess, this is the maiden, and her element is fire for new beginnings, creativity, and metallurgy. She supports fresh endeavors and the magic of the seed's awakening. Willow's color is bright but also silver. Her stone is the moonstone. This lunation is called the Storm Moon.

Willow is the tree of enchantment and mysteries. She is a symbol for the feminine principle, and is ruled by the moon. She promotes and increases our psychic and intuitive powers. She stimulates our intuition, makes our dreams more vivid, and enables us to interpret their messages. Much of my own inner guidance and affirmation has come through my dreams, and history tells of people who received answers to puzzles, blueprints of new inventions, or pieces of music while dreaming.

Willow also encourages and aids in meditation. She increases our visionary skills and offers inspiration and clarity of mind. She helps us explore our inner world and loves prophecy and divination. Willow has an ongoing association with the fine arts, and the muses of creativity. Groves of willows are magical and can inspire poets, writers, artists, and musicians, as well as priestesses.

She reminds us of the ancient goddess in all her aspects of maiden, mother, and crone. She is lithe and supple like the virgin, fertile and prolific like the mother, and wizened and powerful like the crone. Legend says rain was the gift given to her by the Moon Goddess, and indeed, she loves water. Tears are also her gift. Tears bring the release of held-in pain and struggle and are an inborn gift that helps us release our sadness and move through the grieving process.

Willow encourages us to appreciate the entire range of emotions that rise within us. These are all our children and need our attention, love, and understanding. She asks us not to suppress our feelings, but to recognize them and give them a safe place for expression. Healing is always our promised reward once we have cleared the air. Willow desires that we drop our judgments or beliefs that some feelings are unworthy. Willow encourages us to be kind, and to release all emotions, even negative ones. She asks us not to get stuck in this process but to let the feelings go, move on, and understand our inner cycles.

Willow reminds us that there are times when it is best to surrender completely to the watery world of emotions and the subconscious, so that we may be carried toward a deeper understanding of our innermost feelings and our true selves. When we become aware of deeply buried feelings, we wake up and can develop into emotionally healthy people. Willow teaches the consequences of love and loss in matters of the heart. She teaches that emotional expression is our birthright, and that the sharing of feelings of ecstasy and pain can help the human spirit.

We ask Willow to give us strength in understanding the feminine principles of cycle, creativity, community, cooperation, and receptivity. She shows us that our relationships with other women offer profound healing when we share our authentic feelings, without gossip or envy. Willow also enables us to realize that within every loss lies the potential for something new. She restores us after a heavy trial or great loss, enabling forward movement to new ventures. She helps us in co-creation to heal resentment, pain, betrayal, loss, envy, or jealousy. She offers compassion, comfort, new hope, and rebirth.

Healers used the bark of willow to ease illnesses aggravated by cold and damp. Salicylic acid found in the bark and leaves was an early version of aspirin, which comes from another plant, meadowsweet. Wands from willow branches make wonderful protective charms. Willow leaves were used to attract lovers. An old British custom for rejected or abandoned lovers was to wear willow on their hats. To "wear the willow" was to grieve openly—a very brave suggestion, and a healthy one.

Totems, Guides, and Deities

Willow's totems are the bee and the dove. In an age in which many of us lack examples of community or tribes, bees remind us of our need for the collective and the satisfaction that comes from finding our place within a community.

Ancient Sumerian artifacts found in the Middle East depict bee goddesses, who provided comfort, prosperity, nourishment, and well-being to the community. Ancient healing temples provided ritual and healing on every level: psychic, emotional, physical, spiritual, and intellectual. The key elements were those of cooperation and the sharing of resources. Equally important was finding one's place to give and to receive.

In a beehive, the queen bee's health and fertility directly affect the success of the entire colony. Bees show us efficiency, industry, collective awareness, and devotion. They offer a symbol of how we can live and work together. Worker bees are drawn to flowers because of their color and scent, and honey is the result. Honey has provided sweetness and healing throughout the ages, from the ancient Greeks to Native American medicine. It is created through group endeavor and cooperation. I believe we all need more honey in our lives!

The bee community offers us a wonderful pattern for creating health and happiness. Does your connection to the Divine Feminine provide you with the healing and nurturance you desire? Do you have a healing community to support you? Are you providing sweetness to others on a daily basis? Even though our culture does not encourage our connection to the natural world, and even though we are generally taught to be competitive rather than cooperative, it is our choice. Let's build community based on healing, honey, and harmony. What can you do to promote this?

The dove was originally tied to Aphrodite and Astarte, who represented love, passion, and war. Later, the dove came to represent Sophia, goddess of wisdom. Athena was connected to the dove, who represented love and strategy, rather than victory by force. The idea of truce and negotiation is an amazing one; power with, rather than power over, was the symbol of the dove and thus became a symbol of peace. Today, the dove represents cooperation and wisdom, and brings the hope that both sides of an issue or problem can be fairly represented and heard. The dove carrying the olive branch is a powerful symbol of our desire for world peace. We are reminded that because the feminine principle gives birth and raises children, it holds the ultimate desire that no person—certainly no child—should ever die in war.

The Saille/Willow month honors the maiden aspect of the goddess. Symbolized by the crescent moon, this time of year heralds the spark and energy of youth and the seeker. Brigit is one of the maiden goddesses we honor along with Persephone, Pallas Athena, Artemis, and other daughter representatives. This is the time of year to honor our daughters and to mentor younger women. This is also a time to nurture the beginning stages of our dreams and enterprises.

Guided Meditation

Imagine yourself in a beautiful green and grassy field. It is a warm and comfortable early spring day, and you feel a gentle breeze. Walk through the field until you come to a very large weeping willow tree. She is awe-inspiring: huge, yet gentle. Her branches gracefully sweep to touch the ground and you think about the wonderful shade she will provide when the hot months of summer come. Go to her trunk and touch her. Thank her for her majesty. Acknowledge the breath she provides you. Look up and see the sky through her branches. Look down and see the magnitude of her root system. Find a comfortable place to sit as you journey with Willow. Sit with her energy for a short time ... (pause)

In ancient Britain, there was no shame connected with sexuality, menstruation, pregnancy, childbearing, or female independence. These were not reasons to be persecuted or ostracized but reasons to be honored. The willow tree was a positive image of female fertility and power. Lunar rhythms, the menstrual cycle, intuitive giftedness, and the female collective were perceived with dignity. The willow was a joyful and sustaining image. Take a moment to embrace this original perception of Willow and honor her in this light. Be willing to perceive yourself as a woman or man in this same light. Promise Willow that you will always treat her, as well as yourself, with esteem ... (pause) Willow responds—she is thrilled beyond words to be seen in her true nature. She is thrilled beyond words to see *you* in *your* true nature.

As you marvel at her largesse, you reflect on how in modern times, the image of a weeping willow is often seen upon gravestones to express grief. In stories, she often signifies the pain of being born female. Sometimes, she expresses the grief of a woman who is left pregnant and abandoned by her lover, experiencing shame and ostracization from her community. Or perhaps she is the tears of a woman's unfulfilled love and her longing to be free. Willow may represent the loss of a child through illness or accident, abortion, or miscarriage. She might be the voice of the pain of infertility. She may stand for the desperation of physical violence, rape, and abuse. Although you won't turn your back on the suffering women have endured, resolve within yourself today to invoke your power as a healer.

Willow is your staunch ally in healing. She understands how emotion has been suppressed and hidden away because of the attitudes and values you've had to live with. Listen, and she will tell you to value your feelings. If you've experienced crisis or loss, sometimes an emotional numbness sets in, because the feelings are too painful. Willow teaches us that those feelings must be felt and brought to the surface. Emotional release is important; you must move through different levels of sadness and find inner strength and healing from the experience. Her name, Saille, means a sudden outburst of action, expression, or emotion. She asks you to share your heartache with her … (long pause)

Willow honors your deepest feeling and secrets. She is not here to censor you or tell you how you should or shouldn't feel. She accepts everything as natural. Talk to Willow about your joys and grief. If you have a particular need for healing, tell her, and let her great comfort and compassion sweep through you … (long pause)

Willow wants you to take your development further. She wants you to move with the flow of life rather than resist your feelings, and let doubt block you. She teaches that contained within a loss or a betrayal or a disappointment or a struggle is the capacity for growth. She will help you when you have difficulty letting go, and when you suffer adversity and misfortune. She gives herself to help you move you through bitterness, disappointment, betrayal, and loss. She helps soothe the painful feelings of resentment, jealousy, envy, and hatred. Tell her where you feel stuck and let her energy work on you. What are you now able to let go of? … (long pause)

She has courage and energy to share with you. She wants you to be supple and bend with the wind, but not break. She wants you to shed your tears, but not drown in them. She invites you to connect to your inner mystery and stand in your independence and personal power. She asks you to develop your intuition and take seriously your own inner life. She wants you to notice the changes of the moon and feel your own creative cycle.

This is the time of year when plans, new directions, and desires can burst forth toward growth. Willow offers you the magic of that spark that ignites all beginnings. She wants you to listen to your own inner voice, and your nighttime dreams. She encourages you to go deep and give consideration to your heartfelt desires. She invites you to write poems, listen to music, and do creative things. She asks you to use your tools of divination. Listen and receive from Willow. What does she say to you about what you truly desire? What does she reflect back to you? ... (pause)

She says these are the times when humanity's creative spirit and nature can work together for healing on the planet, coming from people who stand together and know they are powerful creators of their own lives. She says both you and she are sacred. From that sacred knowing, you can transform your world—it starts with you. Spend a few minutes with Willow talking about what you wish to create ... (pause)

Stay with Willow for a moment and thank her for her many gifts. Promise her that you will honor her and yourself. When you have finished, bid her farewell. Stand firmly in your own feminine light and honor the particular cycle you are in, whether it be maiden, mother, or crone. Each holds its own virtues. If you are a man, honor the women in your life, and your own feminine side. Then, very gently and very slowly, come back to this time and this space. You can return to Willow anytime you like because she lives inside you. I hope that Willow, in all her grace and power, will never be just another tree to you ever again!

Willow Healing

When you feel troubled, in emotional pain, or very angry, bring Willow's energy in. She will hold you and allow you to accept your feelings so you can release them, and she will offer you comfort. Like Apple, Willow is a great mother.

When your body is aching and in pain, or you have a fever, ask Willow's healing property to assist you. Close your eyes and connect with her, and simply ask for her assistance. Her energy will be transmitted to you and you might feel the pain and fever lessen.

Direct Willow energy to your daughters or to the younger women in your life. She provides strength and the ability to bend without breaking during times of stress or storms. When you are troubled in your relationships with your children, mother, or the women who raised you, ask Willow to intervene.

Sometimes life becomes too demanding. Calm yourself by imagining a huge mother willow tree shading and hiding you under her umbrella. She can provide you a valuable time-out from a hectic life. Sometimes in the midst of caring for others, we forget to care for ourselves.

Invite the goddess Brigit to bless your beginning projects and endeavors. As the muse, she brings inspiration and a spark of creativity. Willow is our enthusiasm, optimism, and excitement. She has the energy to begin things and is full of promise. Take notice of the crescent moon in the sky and watch it grow to its fullness.

Use the ideas in the Willow meditation about manifesting your desires. Any artistic or creative pursuit can release inner emotion and activity. Willow is happiest when we do not hold in or hold back the contents of our inner life. She does not judge our feeling nature. On the contrary, she sees our complex array of feelings as our unique gift, and celebrates it. From our feelings we can write stories, create ceremonies and rituals, paint pictures, plant gardens, knit sweaters, or create anything we can imagine. It is from this inner youthful and vital wellspring that we begin.

Ash

ꝚUɪꝚ–AᴚH

February 21—March 20
5th Lunation, February/March

Description: The ash grows tall; leaves and branches develop in pairs. Each leaf has five to eleven pointed leaflets. The leaves themselves are pointed, serrated, and lined from the central vein to the edges. Small male and female flowers usually grow on separate trees. Ashes drop "keys," or winged fruit that look like canoe paddles. The keys grow late in the season and fall to the ground in autumn. The trunks are usually very rough and textured.

Ogham: Nuin ("nin"), N: ᚅ
The World Tree, inner and outer worlds linked, "As above, so below," macrocosm and microcosm

Class: Chieftain

Rune: Naudhiz, Nauthiz ᚾ
Constraint, necessity, pain, the shadow, struggle, strain, necessary action against restraint or stagnation, shamanism

Totems: The Hanged Man; Dolphin; the Three Fates, or Moræ

Astrology: Pisces, February 18–March 20, ♓
"I believe," a mutable water sign of feminine polarity
Symbol: two fish swimming in opposite directions
Ruling Planet: Neptune ♆, the 12th house of the chart

Body Parts: Rules the feet

Colors: marine greens

Keywords: sensitivity, imagination, intuition, emotional, escapist,
   impressionable, compassionate, sacrificial, dreams and visions,
   merging, unity, oneness, fear

The Nuin/Ash Month

The Ash tree is often called the "World Tree," referring to the myth-ic tree at the center of the world, described in many cultural myths worldwide. In Norse mythology, it is called *Yggdrasil* and is believed to be the center of everything in every dimension. The Norse god Odin hung from it for nine days and nights, and as a result, received visions of what would become the runes and his own enlighten-ment. This month's color is a glassy green, and the lunation is called the Chaste Moon.

In Celtic mythology, Ash was the tree of enchantment and magic. Magic wands were made from ash wood and were used in creat-ing spells. It was understood that spell manifestations were created with respect. The words, "If it harm none, do what you will" and the three-fold rule (that any spell, good or bad, will come back to the spell maker three times over) applied here. Ethics existed, and were simple. Responsibility and stewardship were part of natural law.

Like all the great trees, the ash tree is rooted to the earth, as we are; its branches reach towards heaven. Ash provides us with a pat-tern for our own evolution: we are of the earth and also made of the stars. Both ash and human were made to bridge consciousness from other realms to the physical. We reach into the mysteries so we may continue to evolve as stewards of this planet. Connection with this tree and her totems promises us enhanced understanding and the ex-pansion of our consciousness.

Ash shares the month of March with Pisces and the planet Nep-tune. Higher vibrations of spiritual oneness, unity, forgiveness, heal-ing, and unconditional love take center stage. The panacea of love, a balm for all earthly pain and suffering, is readily available if we but ask. Surrender and compassion are this tree's key words, and it teaches us about receptivity and intuition. Ash trees carry what are known as keys, their winged fruit. However, they can function as spiritual keys as well—keys that open doors into increased conscious-ness and other dimensions of love and support. Truly, Ash spans both the microcosm and the macrocosm of all that is. A reflection of the universe, Ash is the past of Abred, the present of Gwynedd, and the future of Ceugant in Celtic cosmology. She is the cycle of birth, death, and rebirth, and the continuous flow of energy from one form to another, from one dimension into another.

Ash represents the center of all that is, also the center of our-selves. What we retrieve when we take time to notice our inner life can be brought forth from our depths. By bringing to light what has been waiting and hidden, we make active what has slumbered. What is intuited can be shared and brought to light. We can gather what we find in times of quiet receptivity and set our intention for later budding, blossoming. and eventual manifestation. The portal in this month lets us dive deep and find our own wisdom. Once discovered, we can retrieve the gems and rich artifacts of our own souls. When retrieved and honored, these discoveries bring vitality, direction, and purpose and are the gifts that change the world. The only thing re-quired of us is a willingness to use them.

Never think you are one tiny, inconsequential speck of life with-out power and purpose. When you turn away from lies and hurt-ful, self-hating programming and begin to live from your inner fire and inspiration, you affect everything in this world, including other people. Ash offers you a guide for how to accomplish this.

That being said, the process of self-discovery cannot be forced. It takes time and will follow its own course. For the seeker's part, pa-tience and the willingness to bide one's time until secrets are revealed is the path. A bit like limbo, this phase is often experienced as enforced helplessness. No matter what we do, we cannot achieve anything.

This is often known as the "liminal" phase, and feels like everything is out of our hands or that nothing is really happening.

Like Odin's suffering on Yggdrasil, we believe we will never see the light of day or that the dark night of the soul will never end. We may feel like a sacrificial lamb or a scapegoat. From a larger perspective, suffering may be the only means by which we will allow cosmic realization to enter our life. Unfortunately, pain is often a path to a more universal wisdom and leads us to a greater release. Cracks in a well-hardened ego let in the light.

Obstacles we encounter may be of our own making; they may show up in the world around us. They bring difficulty, and we are required to learn to deal with severe restraint. It is said that troubles, denials, and setbacks are our greatest teachers, guides, and allies. Perhaps it is only in times of great darkness that we begin our spiritual journey. As a species, we are stubborn, and it takes much for us to ask for help or to arrive at the conclusion that we are lost. Often it is not until we truly despair that we ask the universe for help. Luckily, the universe will answer our needs if we ask and indicate that we are open to receiving help and direction. The faster we can release our negative emotions, the faster the cosmos can send helpful information.

When fishermen can't go to sea, they repair their nets. In times of forced inaction, we can the mend fences, restore balance, and ponder our lives. We can keep faith alive, calm our anger, and restrain our impulses to wail and act out. We can be modest, humble, and even-tempered, and we can cleanse ourselves. We can love what has been shunned as we reevaluate everything. Sometimes, we figure we might as well, since nothing else seems to work. And when we finally let go and admit we don't know what to do and that we need help, the universe is ready and waiting.

What comes next may differ from our expectations; the inner blueprint does not necessarily follow our plans, despite our best intentions. The next step is arranged through our hearts and our compassion. This is where the mystery comes in, represented by the ash tree nymphs or dryads. They are versions of the three fates. Their number three suggests the triple divinity of the maiden, mother, and crone and the feminine principle. They are our muses, and they know the past, present, and future.

Odin hung upside down nine days on the World Ash and through his trial he accessed the primordial feminine wisdom of the Meliae or Morae. He became all-wise through their transmissions, communications, and empowerments. Woden's (another name for Odin) Day is Wednesday, or Ash Wednesday. If we take off the layers of Christian association, we begin to dig into a heritage of knowledge that transcends time and place. What is the real message in the Ash Wednesday and in Odin's hanging upside down? What will our journey into our hearts and our souls reveal? Here is where the magic and the juice are. Every creative pursuit first comes as the muse. If we pay attention, we are offered help, inspiration, direction, and guidance.

Ash offers to sooth our impatience and restlessness. She will cultivate the quieting down of the mind. She will aid us as we reach into the inner stillness. Ash will facilitate understanding between the various realms of existence. The job of the Ash is to act as a bridge. She transmits information from above and below. She draws from the Earth, from unseen realms, from gods and goddesses, from totems, from the mystery schools of the past, and from the universe and the star nations, and she feeds it to our inner depths. We can take this information from our depths and bring it forth to our minds through emotion and creative inspiration. As we listen to ourselves and are stimulated by poetry and music and art and dance, the whole universe feverently hopes we will become responsible, take the information that reveals itself to us, and translate it into regenerative action and positive activity.

The universe longs for us to know that we are powerful creators. When we choose to create beauty, peace, compassion, and love, we build a new world. The divine feminine principle that supports the building of this new world is found inside. Can we feel what magnificent creatures we are? Ash models a pattern of possibility for us. If we but take the time, we will be richly rewarded.

Totems, Guides, and Deities

The totem of the ash is the dolphin. These creatures are associated with the fabled city of Atlantis and expanded consciousness. Some believe that dolphins have the capacity to communicate with many dimensions and many beings of expanded consciousness. Their great intelligence and their sonar ability allows them to communicate with incredible sensitivity and awareness. As totems, they are known for their joy, unconditional love, and patience. They have a long-suffering air, and are forgiving and accepting. Dolphins are heralded messengers who have agreed to support and encourage humanity on its path towards the evolution of our consciousness. They are willing to help us to understand and accept our responsibility in the role we play in the web of existence. They still believe in us, even when we give up on ourselves.

Dolphins have been known to rescue imperiled humans at sea, a savior quality that amazes us even today. Dolphins are always willing to provide compassionate intervention, even sacrificing themselves so we might gain enlightenment and save ourselves from destruction.

In the past, the matriarchal Minoan culture of the Mediterranean Sea honored the dolphin in art and sculpture. The month of March is sacred to Poseidon, whose sea chariot is drawn by dolphins. Bronze Age Greek writings mention a feminine "Poseideia," possibly the earliest form of this deity. Cretan funeral urns were shaped like wombs and pictured dolphins, representing the soul's journey to other realms. The mother of all Greek sea goddesses is Eurynome, famous for her appearance as a half-woman, half-dolphin. We are honoring the mother aspect of the goddess here and the power of her ability to procreate.

Another aspect of the goddess is her ability to see the future. The priestesses at Delphi (womb) inhaled gases emitted from the crevices in the rocks beneath the temple. These intoxicating fumes allowed for vision within a trance state that gave priestesses oracular abilities. Neptune and Pisces are related to intoxication and trance state through the use of hallucinogenic substances like plants and alcohol. However, I don't advocate use of such substances for recreational use or escapism—they often lead to addiction and abuse. In ancient Greece, use of these substances was controlled and held as sacred within special rites and rituals, as it was in cultures the world over. Hallucinogens were used to enable a person to travel from one state of perception to another. Although there are still shamans and healers who do use substances for spiritual ceremony and healing, we of the modern world have lost the ability to use these substances in a holy, respectful way and it has led us to the destruction of our psyches.

Although we can no longer physically find the oracle at Delphi, we can receive messages from her and her totems. More importantly, we do not have to use substances in order to enter trance states. If we are open, many of the beings who dwell in different dimensions are willing to transmit messages. We can interact with them simply with our intention; taking time to quiet the mind and internally dialogue with them is for our benefit, and is done out of love.

The character of the dolphin is like the Ash in that it will support us in our difficult situations, or in any self-imposed inaction (like the Hanged Man). Remember that dolphins will buoy us up, and keep us afloat as we tread water. Use this month to confer with them, to look at things from a totally different perspective. When our lives are turned upside down, we can choose to look at the experience with more acceptance and understanding. Noticing and observing the opportunity to change is a gift. Whether we make quiet time in our lives to listen to our inner muse or life knocks us flat on our backs, we can know we are supported in our process as we approach new understanding. Dolphin is our biggest fan—full of joy, faith, and encouragement.

The message of the Hanged Man in the tarot is relevant to this portal. He hangs upside down, looking at things (situations) from a different perspective. Reality consensus is often an agreed-upon lie, and the Hanged Man asks us to stop for a moment and reconsider. Stop the doing. Stop the rushing. He asks us to take time out to really question the nature of things around us. When imitating his posture, the blood rushes to the head and the brain is stimulated and invigorated with oxygen. Here is a breath of fresh air, new wisdom, and possibility.

Odin, as powerful and masculine as he was, still found himself hung upside down from the World Tree. All people have periods in their lives when they are stopped dead in their tracks. Interruption can come in the loss of a loved one, the end of an important love relationship, the loss of a job, or a sudden illness. Odin (the Hanged Man) shows us he is willing to remain suspended, literally and mentally. He surrenders to the process and ignores the analytical workings of the left brain. He asks us to question the mind's need for interpretation and control, surrenduring to the domain of the feminine principle—honoring intuition, receptivity, and quiet.

In the Hanged Man's period of suspension, we invite in our deepest feelings and inner knowing. If we can stop the mental chatter and our need for business, we can relax, listen for that small voice within, or follow a thread of emotion and longing we never pay attention to. How else can we discern between meaningless habitual or culture-based programming and our own deepest desires?

Guided Meditation

In your mind's eye, travel to a place at the very center of the world. When you arrive, you see a tree marking the spot. You may sense that the tree lives inside you and is growing at the very place where you meet your soul. Take a moment to really connect with your tree. Notice the shape of the tree, its size, the strength of its trunk, and its foliage. This is the tree of yourself at the center of the world.

You begin to notice the story of your life imprinted upon the tree. You see the times that were difficult for you, and the lessons you learned. Notice any gnarled places where the story tells of wounding, bitterness, despair, or a sense of futility. Also notice your joys and achievements. Really take this in and closely examine your tree... (pause) As your story approaches this moment in time, notice any stuck places or difficulties. Notice also as the tree branches out to new possibilities. Notice how the sun begins to shine through the branches as they reach up to the sky. Be aware of the steady growth of your tree.

While you stand there watching your tree, three tree nymphs come into view to communicate with you. There is a maiden, a mother, and a wise old crone. They are dancing and merry, and you enjoy watching them interact with each other. They come to stand with you to honor your inner tree. They remark on its beauty, and you too begin to feel the beauty and presence of this tree.

Looking into the heart of your tree, you form a connection with your own heart. As you honor your central flame, you feed it with love; as you do this, your heart flame grows and fills you with warmth and appreciation. Listen very carefully for that small central voice at the core of yourself. Listen to its messages and to its concerns. Simply lend your ear ... (pause)

Be willing to quiet your mind so concerned with judgments, comparisons, and analysis. Be willing to surrender yourself to beauty, peace, harmony, and love. Try to recall music, songs, books, or poems that have moved you. Try to recall what has inspired you. Think for a moment about what really feeds you and what you most enjoy. Here at the center, you find inspiration, the courage to be yourself, and the ability to connect with your own heart. Take a moment to remember who you are and what you truly love ... (pause)

At this time, the tree nymphs surround you in a circle and sing you their special song. You become filled with their special magic. They are the three fates that spin your story. Let them know what you want to happen in the next chapter of your life. Communicate these intentions from this deepest place, from your heart's desires; if the tree of yourself here could speak, what would it request ... (pause)

As the journey concludes, give your gratitude to the tree spirits. Honor your world tree and let it know that you intend for it to thrive. Embrace the next chapter of your life that you have begun to create, and feel the power of possibility and intention towards your greater good. Be prepared to share the results of whatever may come in the future—it is the fruit that grows from your own tree. Now, gently come back into this time and place, and after grounding and centering, write your experiences in your journal.

Ash Healing

Call the energy of Ash when you need to find your center. Draw a circle and draw a tree inside it as a way of reconnecting with your central inner place. A circle (in this case, a mandala, or sacred circle) represents unity, on many levels of consciousness. Become the tree in your imagination and allow its strength to steady you. Ground and center within the image of this tree.

I have kept mandala journals for years. Whenever I have the time, I place a circle upon a blank page and put designs and images into it or make a collage. Soon I have a pictorial account of my journey; it is deeply moving, reassuring, and a powerful personal symbol. You may want to place the tree that you are focusing on every month within a mandala or create a tree collage within a mandala and place it upon your altar as a focusing device and as a way to show your gratitude for a particular tree. Remember, it is attention given that acts as your entrance fee into other realms.

When you seek understanding and wish to bring light to confusion, ask for this tree's guidance. Ash will link you to universal knowing. It will help you understand that your thoughts, feelings, and actions play a part in moving the world towards a vision of peace and harmony. Every effort on your part vibrates outwardly on every level. Ash tree will help you understand your life in a wider context. Any problems or difficulties can be met within this larger worldview, and Ash helps you find your place in the grand scheme of things.

When you feel alone, isolated, or overwhelmed, call forth Ash's energy. Imagine yourself sitting under its tall umbrella of branches and leaves, with your back leaning against its firm trunk. Feel its strong roots connecting you to the earth, feel the trunk supporting your body, and feel its branches and leaves stretching up to the sky and the cosmos. You were made this way too, and this tree will connect you to a body sense of knowing that you are part of the whole and that you are never alone.

When you feel fate is going in the wrong direction, travel to your central tree and invite the three fates to sit in counsel with you. Tell them your concerns and negotiate strategies for new outcomes. Be open to their counsel—they are the representatives of your own wisdom, intuition, and knowing.

This tree and its totems can be especially helpful in addressing any substance abuse or addiction. Ash can also be helpful in any addiction recovery process. One reason for addiction is to stave off or avoid pain. We often self-medicate to ease our suffering even if we are unconscious of it. Why work through difficult emotional problems when a pill popped in your mouth can provide instant relief? Truthfully, the unconditional love offered through this tree and her helpers can calm the spirit and act as a balm for suffering, not just dampen and mute it for a while. Enlist Ash in your recovery program. She can restore the otherwise eroded senses of self-worth and self-love.

Become familiar with the runes as oracles and guides. Gather stones and put images of the runes upon them. Store them in a special pouch. This is a great way to learn the meaning of the runes over time. Purchase a deck of tarot cards. Study them, getting to know the deep symbolism and subtle lessons of each card. Work your way towards doing spreads, first for yourself, then for others.

Pay attention to your dreams; write down anything you remember right after waking up. Recording your nighttime visions is one way your inner tree sends you guidance. Keep track of which totems, guides, and deities show up for you.

Call on the energies of the planet Neptune and the astrological sign of Pisces. These energies can dissolve tension and reconnect you with the invigoration of source energy. Their greatest message is one of unity consciousness and love. Gather together with like-minded people and create rituals and ceremonies together. Become involved in a community-based project to helps others. Doing for others is an important part of creating balance in our lives.

HUATHE–HAWTHORN

March 21–April 17
6th Lunation, April

Description: The trunks can be slightly twisted; they have a gnarly, feisty quality about them. Trunk size is usually small and slender, but they can grow quite large. Leaves are small and rounded and have a trefoil shape with a pointed end. Hawthorns bear red berries ("haws") in autumn, and bloom in red, pink, or white flowers in the spring. The branches have prominent thorns.

Ogham: Huathe ("hoh'uh" or "OO-ah"), H: ⊣
Cleansing, chastity, purity, protection of inner realm, preparation for Beltane

Class: Peasant

Holiday: March 21, Spring Equinox, Alban Eiler

Rune: Hagalaz [H]
Mother Rune, disruption for the purpose of awakening, sudden occurrences, seed beginning to grow underground, new growth

Totems: Fairies, White Stag, Unicorn, Herne the hunter (an aspect of Cernunnos, the antlered god), King Arthur, the sacred marriage between intellect/mind and feeling/intuition

Hawthorn

Astrology: Aries, March 20–April 19, ♈
    "I am," a cardinal fire sign of masculine polarity
    Symbol: the ram
    Ruling Planet: Mars ♂
    Body Part: Rules the head
    Colors: reds and purples
    Keywords: aggressive, assertive, straightforward, adventurous,
        impulsive, active, physical, action-oriented

The Huathe/Hawthorn Month

Other names for the hawthorn are the haeg thorn, whitethorn, quick-thorn, the bread and cheese tree, and the may tree. Hawthorn represents cleansing, purity, and chastity in preparation for union and rebirth. This month was an important preparatory period in which ancient Britons anticipated the great rite at Beltane on May 1. This month gives us pause and beckons us to clean up our act, to let go of what no longer serves, and to treat our bodies, minds, and souls with sacred respect. This month's color is purple, and the lunation is called the Seed Moon.

Despite the jubilant celebration of spring's arrival, this month is a time to quiet oneself and go within. As it relates to the rune, chastity does not necessarily refer to sexual abstinence, although it certainly may be included in one's purification. Instead, it refers to personal sovereignty in which we reclaim our personal power and pay attention to our own inner life. Fasting, ritual cleansing, and refraining from one's usual habits and patterns is encouraged. We may want to seek retreat and silence in order to reconnect with the divine and the unseen worlds.

The sacred feminine is represented in the image of a virgin maiden in a virgin forest. Her companion is the unicorn, another strong symbol of purity, resting its head upon her lap. While the image might call to mind fairy tales, it really places the mystery of sensuality and sexuality under the umbrella of the sacred. Ancients taught that sexuality and spirituality were one. Priestesses of old often served in sacred sexual healing rituals, offered to men who came home from war with broken hearts and spirits after so much brutality and carnage.

These sacred women were unmarried, and therefore free to tend to their spiritual connection and evolution. They developed the songs, dances, rituals, and sexual rites that provided healing and wholeness to their communities. They were the ceremonialists, musicians, entertainers, philosophers, healers, and keepers of the sacred teachings. They tended the hearth of the great mysteries, and had direct communication with the muses and the great mother. Their purpose was to seek renewal and the continuation of a healthy, harmonious, and balanced world infused with the spirit of nature and the divine.

In the time prior to May 1, we are reminded to spend time alone with ourselves. Attention to our relationship with ourselves, nature, and the divine is essential for maintaining our sovereignty, and is a way to ensure power over our own lives. Hawthorn calls for a personal time-out, retreat, or clearing. The notion of spring cleaning comes from the notion of such reflection and renewal.

Hawthorn is often planted as a hedge to provide a fence or barrier, as the thorns protect against unwanted or invading influences. This tree is the great guardian of the integrity of our interior space and is also the faerie tree. Though faeries are widely believed to not exist, Hawthorn maintains a protected sphere for the magical realm.

I once lived with two beautiful hawthorn trees, planted on either side of the walkway leading up to my front door. I was delighted with the protection and merriment these trees provided me and felt the faeries' presence. My small daughter and I often left little presents of food and drink under those hawthorns. For magical use, Hawthorn can be called upon to encircle and protect sacred spaces and events.

At this time of year, we concentrate on blending the element of fire, which represents new thought, inspiration, and action, with the element of water, which represents emotion, feelings, and the heart.

Actions are wedded to feeling, the will to the heart. The pure white flowers of the Hawthorn represent the new idea ready to be infused with spiritual fertilization, so things of worth may be born, grown, and manifested. The red haws that appear in autumn remind us to harvest that which was created from our original action.

Hawthorn's message is thus: "We anchor the world of mystery and magic to your world. We are sacred. We protect the temple. We remind you to keep yourself sacred. The faeries love us and we love the faeries. We welcome you to the world of enchantment."

Totems, Guides, and Deities

As mentioned earlier, Hawthorn is a faerie tree. The hawthorn month is a wonderful time to honor the elemental kingdom. When the news told of our military's plans to occupy Iraq after the terrorist attacks on September 11, I felt profound sadness, and turned to the faeries and angels for help. Through words that came internally, they informed me I didn't have the full scope or the bigger picture. I was told that our job as a species is to work on purifying what we create with our negative thoughts, words, and deeds. I believe much of the pollution on the planet is really from the negativity and fear we continually generate on an energetic level. The unseen elemental spirits work constantly to clean things up, as do certain animals, absorbing what we create. This inner communication I received made me aware of the invisible helpers who circle the globe and work to neutralize this negativity all the time. Even the frogs and dragonflies work hard, making sounds to break up the heaviness of human influence. Our belief in fairies helps encourage them. When you can, give them a little thank-you. I don't believe we have any idea how much they do to keep our world alive and well.

Since becoming more conscious of their work and offering my gratitude, I have noticed many fairy rings (mushroom circles) growing abundantly in my yard. I urge you to think of the elves, leprechauns, gnomes, and pixies. Delight with the faeries and sylphs, fireflies and the salamanders, and the goddesses who hold the master plans for the flowers, trees, and plants—they are responsible for overseeing the growth and care of every plant in our world. We take it for granted that the food we eat grows in the earth, and are unaware of these helpers who nurture and care for the plant life on which we rely.

I am also grateful to the mystical creatures such as dragons, unicorns, and mermaids that live in hidden worlds. Every creature of "myth" is part of the fabric of our world. Light beings and angels of all kinds exist as well. And there are bands of consciousness from beyond the stars that feed us with their advanced levels of love and wisdom. Give thanks to the angels and divine beings that guide and guard us.

The goddess of the hawthorn is the virgin maiden. Her steady companion is the magical unicorn. Treasure your innocence and do not judge your naiveté; it is your return to the magic of your childhood that opens you to receive communications from other realms. All daughters are honored here. Here, we honor the period of time usually referred to as a latency period, before a child becomes pubescent. This is a time of honoring childhood, yet preparing for the budding of sexual identity.

It may sound contradictory, but the maiden's purity and unspoiled beauty are not separate from her burgeoning sexuality. The act of creation is nature's greatest gift. Be happy for your own sensuality and sexuality, as these are sacred gifts from the goddess. Persephone (also known as Kore) returns from the underworld and her mother, Demeter, allow the world to flower in her joy.

Herne is the hunter aspect of Cernunnos, the antlered god. He identifies with his prey and honors them for their sacrifice—sustenance for other life forms. Herne is the archetype for the sacred realization of the interconnectedness of the life and death cycles. He teaches us to identify with the things we eat, and to give gratitude for the sacrifice, be it plant or animal. Herne is an important part of the masculine mystery.

Another totem for Hawthorn is the great white stag of the forest. This awesome creature serves as a reminder of the magical nature of our world and ourselves. It appeared rarely—in times of holy union. Whether it is with a lover, idea, project, or a ritual with oneself, the white stag lets us know we are on holy ground. The sacred marriage occurs when intellect and feeling, mind and intuition, fire and water, and male and female communicate and join together. Here we find wholeness with the union of opposites. The white stag represents this wholeness.

Herne hunts the stag and places the antlers upon his head. In this moment, he becomes Cernunnos, the Horned God. He identifies totally with the power of this grand animal that sacrifices its life. At Beltane, he mates with the Great Goddess to ensure the promise of new life at next year's Beltane. As summer arrives, he flourishes as the Green Man, sacrificing himself for the autumn harvest, celebrated at Lammas. He is sacrificed as the crops are cut and gathered and the seeds are stored for the winter. He is the master of the cycle of death and rebirth in the Wheel of the Year. He will return in the spring to ensure that all life begins again.

Guided Meditation

Begin by grounding and centering, bringing your focus within. Close your eyes and take a few cleansing breaths. Concentrate on your heart and feed it with love. Notice as warmth begins to spread outwards from your heart in every direction. Breathe the energy of the earth into your heart. Breathe into your heart the energy of the sun. Inhale the two energies and allow them to meet at your solar plexus. As you exhale, express cleansing energies from your field.

With your inner sight, imagine a field that hosts a lovely grove of hawthorn trees. It is early spring and the sun is shining. It feels good to be outdoors again and feel the sun's warmth. The trees are blooming with red, pink, and white flowers, and you notice a special aura around the grove, even from afar. As you near the grove, time and space seem to change, and you feel inexplicably giddy, ready to jump and frolic with joy. You enter into the grove and hear the sound of many little beings dancing and frolicking. They do not seem surprised by your presence—in fact, they beckon you to join them. You hesitate momentarily, and decide to sit down and enjoy the festivities from the sideline; you need time to adjust to your new environment and the intense magic nature of this place.

You are able to watch as the faeries, elves, leprechauns, pixies, sprites, and other small creatures dance and sing. You see their individual features and their unique expressiveness. Around the circle of celebration, you see other magical creatures join the party. A unicorn comes to watch and the white stag stands strong and steady. Soon, Herne the Hunter joins the group but has his bow and arrows neatly peace-bound on his back—he has come to be part of the fun. The Green Man and Pan, the gods of the forests, soon also join. Little fairies fly in the air above, as do fire sprites and fireflies. At a little pool within the grove sit mermen and mermaids strumming their harps, and the undines (water sprites) dive in and out of a little waterfall that flows from the rocks. The area within the grove is alive with activity, merriment, and sound. This is a place of magic not within time or space as you know it. Simply be willing to enjoy the enchantment and wonder, and feel the life-giving vigor of this energy.

Soon, the maiden of the grove approaches you. She has beautiful golden hair and a pair of faerie wings, and is dressed in a soft white gown. Upon her head is a princess crown of flowers giving off a sweet perfume. She bows to you and you rise to greet her. There is an incredible sense of safety and joy in this place. She has a hawthorn-flowered crown in her hand and places the crown upon your head. When she places the wreath on your head, you too feel like a fairy or a magical princess. She invites you to join her in a lovely dance to the soulful tune of elfin fiddle players.

When the dance is complete, everyone sits down to rest and have a chat. The beings here very much want to assure you that yes, this dimension is real, although usually hidden from humans. The inhabitants of this grove have things to tell you about their particular jobs and responsibilities within the growing cycle of the planet's flora. Some want to let you know about their job of clearing negativity. Others urge you to believe in magic as you used to when you were a child. Many tell you to look for their signs in mushroom circles and in the fast-flitting movements you see out of the corner of your eye. They let you know that the hummingbirds, dragonflies, butterflies, and even frogs in your backyard are a reminder that magic exists. Take a moment to listen to their messages for you … (pause)

Their last message to you is to remember them. They ask you to support wild places where they can be free and not bothered by human civilization. In addition, they ask for your gratitude; theirs is a large task without recognition. These enchanted friends hint that perhaps there is a little corner of your own yard or garden you could leave wild for them.

Hawthorns in the grove begin to sway and whisper to you. They ask you to consider their thorns—a reminder to protect that which is most sacred to you. These trees let you know that they will protect you from harm and keep safe your vulnerabilities. Are you willing to honor your belief in the unseen world? Give your gratitude for the important work these creatures do in the creation and maintenance of life on Earth. The creatures of this realm reflect that it does no good to argue with humans who are unable to believe in this unseen dimension—but those who do believe are truly blessed.

It is now time for you to leave this special place. Again, give your gratitude and love to each and every creature and express thanks to the hawthorns. Know that you can return to this magical place anytime you want. As you say your goodbyes, return your attention to your own time and place. Bring your attention back into your body, and ground and center. When you feel ready, open your eyes and record your journey in your journal.

Hawthorn Healing

The period before May 1 is a good time for cleansing and purification. You might choose a day of voluntary silence, fasting, or rest in order to prepare for Beltane. Inner work and solitude is supported during this month.

This is a good time for spring cleaning and letting go of old things you no longer use or that have little meaning to you anymore. Prepare to make room for the new, leaving space for what you want to create or manifest in your life. Consider that others may be able to use the things that you no longer need or want. If you find you hoard things and have too much abundance in your environment, try to get some support for letting go of things. Ask a trusted friend to help you. Start small and move from room to room. Buying too much and storing too much can be a sign of suppressed emotion; it would be better to face and heal what is truly bothering you. If you feel too much anxiety or other strong negative feelings about the prospect of clearing your living space, consider professional help.

Touching a hawthorn tree can help you reach a deeper spiritual understanding of your life. This tree will also help you find the love in your heart again, open your heart to others, and liberate your ability to love all (yourself included). You can reclaim your own positive flow of love and energy. Hawthorn refreshes you with hope, joy, innocence, and a sense of renewed fun and merriment.

When you need strong boundaries in a situation or relationship, energetically and in your imagination, plant a hedge of hawthorn shrubs around yourself, or even full-grown trees. This visualization offers wonderful protection—nothing unwanted or harmful can penetrate this. As a meditation exercise, go back into your past and re-create situations that negatively affected you. Bring your present, adult self to the picture and have that strong self advocate for you. You may even take your past self out of the situation completely.

In a guided visualization, I was able to return to an early childhood home and take myself, as an infant, out of my crib and prevent a negative situation that was about to occur. My proof that something very healing had happened occurred with the sudden flow of my menstrual cycle. Usually, I would have intense cramps and it would take days for the process to begin. I felt joyful and relieved in a very palatable way. Using this visualization magic method, the unconscious is willing to "adapt" the new story and release the energy previously held there. Ask Hawthorn to protect you in this process and to ground and transmute the energy release.

Read stories, poems, and fairy tales about the little people. Gather pictures of the flower faeries: they will be grateful and flow their delightful sense of mirth your way. Write your own fairy tale. Who knows—with the proper attitude and gratitude, you may see a faerie!

Oak

DUIR—OAK

April 18—May 15 June 10 - Jul. 7
7th Lunation, April/May June/July

Description: The familiar oak grows from the acorn. It can grow to be an enormous tree with a long life span. Its leaves vary but they all keep to a similar shape. The sides of the leaf are differentiated into three or four extensions with an extension at the end. Sometimes these are rounded and sometimes they are pointed. The trunk is usually strong and wide.

Ogham: Duir ("der," "dur," "doo-er"), D: ⊣
Strength, stability, solid protection and grounding, doorway to the mysteries, fertility, spring, survival, thresholds, ancient knowledge

Class: Chieftain

Holiday: ~~Beltane, May Day, May~~ 1

Rune: Dagaz ᛞ
Breakthroughs, radical transformation, disintegration of old forms, survival after the darkness, success, a new generation, doorways and thresholds

Totems: the bull, Venus, Mother Earth, Persephone, the daughter or maiden archetype, rabbits or hares, eggs

Astrology: Taurus, April 19–May 20 ♉

"I have," a fixed earth sign of negative polarity

Symbol: the bull

Ruling Planet: Venus ♀, the 2nd house

Body Parts: Rules the throat, cerebellum, and back part of the brain

Colors: pink and blue

Keywords: possessive, stable, loyal, determined, powerful, practical, materialistic, sensual, artistic, beauty, comfort

The Duir/Oak Month

This month, we honor the oak tree and the energy of Beltane. The festival of Beltane (Beltain, Beltaen, amongst other spellings) occurs on May 1 (right in the middle of this lunar month), and honors the sacred marriage and the conception of new life. The seed is fertilized and sprouts new life. The colors for this month are black and dark brown, in addition to the pink and blue associated with this month's astrological sign, Taurus. Security and strength are the gifts from this tree. This lunation is called the Hare Moon and represents fertility.

This tree represents great stamina and generation. It is amazing how an oak can grow to become such a huge umbrella of a tree from its tiny acorn! Oak carries the consciousness of our ancestors, who knew how to live in harmony with the cycles of nature. These trees are noble and steadfast, and can help us center. They offer great peacefulness and are the quiet watchers of the world. Oak retains all the memories of ceremony, celebration, education, ancient knowledge, and divination through the ages and through our lineages; they are the great "rememberers."

The Celtic word for oak is *Duir* (also believed to be the word for "door"). Indeed, there are many stories of doorways into huge oak trees. Through such doors, we can journey into the center of the world, or ourselves. Often, doorway visualization was an initiation process involving a task or teaching. Once a pupil had mastered the doorway, they were able to move forward in their lessons of self-knowledge and empowerment. I think of Alice falling into Wonderland through the rabbit hole in the oak tree. We can travel through the oak door to seek self-knowledge.

If you have a chance, sit with an oak tree and ask her for clearing—Oak is excellent at clearing negativities we create in ourselves. She can help you clear away anything you find yourself stuck in or with. Tell her what you desire to manifest and she will help: if you feel unsure about yourself, or worry you might get distracted or carried away, know that Oak offers strong grounding and courage.

As you might expect, oak trees offer sacred space not only for you but for many other creatures and life forms. Offering the oak tree gratitude is energetically helpful. All sentient beings enjoy being thanked and feel encouragement when acknowledged. In return, Oak will offer you wisdom.

In early times, Oak invited and ensured the progeny of all life. Conception was celebrated and represented the union of opposites seen in light and dark, receptivity and action, male and female, and the sun and the moon. Anytime a sacred marriage occurred the mythic White Stag appeared, combining opposing polarities, allowing for personal integration. Seeds of this union are creativity and the release of potential energy. What is honored is the convergence of polarities that explode into a third form which is from the two, but is neither. Three is a magical number and a sacred pattern for manifestation.

Totems, Guides, and Deities

The totem for this month is the bull, the sign of Taurus. Venus is its ruler, and governs aesthetics, beauty, relationships, love, and comfort. The bull offers the power and determination of a fixed earth sign, and lends stability and strength. Like Ferdinand, the rose-smelling bull of the beloved children's book, we are reminded of the bull's gentle and loving side, but also reminded these creatues can be provoked into anger if a threat is perceived.

The bull symbol of ancient times represented one who was willing to put his strength to use in the building of what the lady (Empress or Queen) required for the health and welfare of her people, but also represented aesthetic appeal, as seen in the construction of the Great Pyramids of Egypt. This was the bull's role in the Venus-ruled Age of Taurus, occurring from approximately 4525 to 1875 BCE. At this time, several cultures formed bull-worshipping cults, such as in Minoa (Crete), Assyria, and of course, Egypt. Their sky goddess, Nut, is often seen as a great cow feeding the earth from her udders.

We combine the energies of the wand and fire to work with the qualities of the coming tree months: Oak, Holly, and Hazel. Embracing the qualities of wands (whose element is fire, and direction is south), we bring in passion, aliveness, and creativity. Here we embrace our creative pursuits. Sculpture, pottery, jewelry making, painting, and the performance arts are all examples. We long to take the fire of our inspiration and create beautiful and tangible things on this plane.

The making of a child is also part of the great dance. Beltane was the great fire festival of the year and marked the power of conception. The symbolic mating of the Horned God with the Goddess ensured the thriving and ample harvest for another year of sustenance.

Couples made love in ancient fields to ensure the sprouting of the seeds. Sexuality and sensuality were honored and encouraged. All children born from such unions were cared for with great love and thought to be very special indeed. Symbolically, the maiden walked through the door of her own sexuality, offering herself to her first sexual experiences and the possibility of moving on to the next stage of the triple Goddess—Mother. Imagine a world in which one's first sexual experience was supported and nurtured, and offered in a sacred context. Intercourse was a joyful, happy, fun, exhilarating, and ecstatic experience.

On May Day, we honor the Earth (Taurus' element) and all the plants and flowers in making May baskets. We also honor the sensual and sexual energy of this time of year, and the conception of new life all around us. We give our gratitude for another revolution of the cycle of birth and abundance. We've made it through another winter! This is a time for celebration and conception. What is it you desire to begin?

Guided Meditation

Envision yourself in a grove of oak trees. Feel the strength emanating from these great beings and let their grandness flow into you, affirming the planet's life-giving force. As you take in the power coursing through you, let it invigorate every cell of your body and aspect of your mind.

From within the circle of trees, a beautiful priestess steps forward. Welcome the druidess, knower of the secrets of Earth. She brings peace, stability, productivity, and growth. Allow her to share this bounty with you as she places a garland of flowers around your neck. Smell the delicious fragrances. Experience the awe of this moment with the deity, and acknowledge the calm certainty of the priestess as she stands before you. Look into her eyes and give her your gratitude. She will transmit love and information to you as you listen to her song. (If you like, you may play any music here that connects you with the Goddess.)

The preistess takes your hand and shows you a doorway built into a huge oak tree standing in the grove. She indicates the doorway that leads into the center of the world—the center of yourself. Enter…

You enter the magnificent core; it glistens like a jewel set in a ring of precious metal. Take a moment to sit within this crystalline cave and experience the multi-faceted display of light and color. This is your essential self—your strength, stamina, and authority. Herein lie the secrets of your survival, your endurance, and your ability to adjust to the stresses in your life. This wonderful place is the source of what carries you forward, certain in the knowledge that you will survive and that you can accommodate change and keep going. Take your time as you receive the power and beauty of this place within yourself ... (pause) You may receive a gift or a symbol, a memory or a color ... (pause) When you feel complete, give your gratitude.

Step out of the oak tree through the doorway, back to the grove. The priestess is there to meet you. Know that you will retain the magic of this moment forever. She points to a unique tree; is that your name you see written in the bark? What variety of tree is it? This is your special tree that will always be your special guide and helper; this tree will share her medicine with you. Take a moment to to identify her and take in her spirit. Commune with her ... (pause) Be sure to thank the tree and let her know you will make an effort to study her or meditate with her.

You sense it is time to return to your present time and space. Sincerely thank the druidess, your tree, and the grove. Take a moment to retrieve any messages or gifts. The priestess stands to face you and gives you a kiss on both cheeks, an act of love and gratitude you return. Very slowly, return to your body. Wiggle your toes and feet, pat your legs and thighs, and feel your body on the chair you're sitting in, or the floor supporting you, if you were lying down. When you have returned, open your eyes, and ground and center. Write your experiences in your journal.

Oak Healing

Whenever you feel weak and helpless, sit with an oak or conjure one in your mind. Oak medicine will bring you strength, courage, and bravery.

Oak is grounded and strong. It will help you when you are overly excited, anxious, or nervous. With this tree's help, your energy will ground and even out. When you are carrying too much on your shoulders, you can ask an oak tree to take on the energy and properly disperse it back to the earth for its regeneration.

When you are in a situation that seems to be dragging on or is otherwise stagnant, invite in Oak energy; she will show you that growth and change happen even when you can't tell physically. She grows slowly and steadily from the acorn, sometimes for centuries. She will help you to be patient.

Use the image of the acorn for new ideas, projects, and intentions. Plant them and nourish them well, knowing that in time, a tree will grow forth.

Oak represents fertility. If you are hoping to become a parent, commune with this tree. Ask her to share her powers of fertility.

When you are seeking knowledge, information, guidance, or wisdom, ask Oak for what you need. Expect that synchronicities, situations, people, communications, dreams, and books will appear to answer your questions and needs. Oak responds to specific questions when you are researching something, especially if it has to do with ancient wisdom or spiritual lineages.

Holly

TINNE~HOLLY

May 16—June 12
8th Lunation, May/June

Description: Holly has prickly leaves that stick and hurt. The leaves are quite green and shiny. They also have red berries that grow, even in winter. These trees can grow quite large.

Ogham: Tinne ("chihn'uh," "CHIN-yuh"), T: ᚈ
Justice, balance, polarity and duality brought into wholeness, bringing opposites together, paternity and fatherhood, action

Class: Peasant

Rune: Tiwaz ⬆
Warrior, masculine, direct action, the spear of the warrior or shaman, the art of negotiation, self-surrender for the common good

Totem: Swan, Leda, Lugh and Lucina, Holle and Pluto, The Lovers tarot card, the twins

Astrology: Gemini, May 20–June 20 or 21, ♊
  "I think," a mutable air sign with neutral polarity
  Symbol: the twins Castor and Pollux
  Ruling Planet: Mercury, ☿, the 3rd house
  Body Parts: Rules nervous system, hands, shoulders, arms, lungs
  Colors: nearly all
  Keywords: versatile, flexible, sociable, dualistic, curious, talkative, communicative, impulsive

The Tinne/Holly Month

Holly was a sacred tree to ancient Celts, considered the winter abode for the wood spirits (dryads) and one that ensured protection against ill fortune. Holly offers a defiant life-energy even in the face of winter, when she grows her red berries to let us know her energy is still vital. Planted near a house, Holly offers protection. Holly's color is dark gray. This lunation is called the Dryad Moon.

Tinne/Holly is a warrior. Celts used the wood from this tree to make spears. Lleu, Llew, or Lugh are names for the ancient Celtic hero who acted as the spearman and protector. Llew is also associated with thunder and lightning, as the root word comes from *lu*, meaning light, lucid, luminous, illuminator and translucence. Holly is sacred to these lords of thunder and lightning.

Holly is a champion and a protector, loyal to those who require her protection. While she is compassionate to those who are vulnerable or victimized, justice is also important to Holly, as is the vindication of rights and clarification of claims and grievances. She protects against all negativity, including that which is self-generated and that which comes from others and is aimed to harm us. She guards against potential dangers. What is it you need to be a warrior about? What do you need protection from?

Holly increases love, encourages the positive, and brings good luck. She encourages healing through the protection and sustenance of love in the community.

She offers balance and directness. Holly helps you find the strongest argument in your battle, providing that the fight is just and not directed toward aggression and acquisitiveness. Holly can provide you with the raw energy to restore direction in your life. What do you need strengthened and resolved?

Totems, Guides, and Deities

The goddess of Holly is Holle, guardian of the underworld and keeper of the knowledge of hidden places. She embodies all three aspects of the Goddess, but in particular reigns over death and regeneration. She embodies the same intense energy of her Greco-Roman counterpart, Hades (Pluto). She is mistress of your deadly fears, your dark twin and your shadow self. Another deity is Lugh, god of light, and his counterpart is Lucina, goddess of clarity and vision, justice and insight. Together, light and dark forces make a whole. The twin aspects of duality are brought together in relationship under Gemini.

Holly's totem is the mute swan, mated for life, fearlessly protective of its mate, young, or territory. When its young are threatened, nothing can become quite as ferocious as a swan, yet few creatures are as loving and devoted. Even a swan's shape suggests duality: the body is womb-shaped and the characteristically long neck (in its defensive posture) is phallic-looking.

Tinne/Holly month is associated with Gemini. There are many myths about the Gemini twins Castor and Polydeuces (Pollux to the Romans), who had undying love for each other. After Polydeuces received a mortal wound, Castor intervened so they wouldn't be separated forever, and begged Zeus for mercy. Zeus gave them a compromise: half a year in the underworld and the other half on Mount Olympus, home to the gods and goddesses. Unfortunately, Castor was mortal, and Polydeuces immortal (they shared a mother, but had different fathers). When Castor became old, nearing death, it was Polydeuces this time who asked Zeus (his father) to save his brother. Zeus placed both of them in the sky together, and they were transformed into the Gemini constellation.

In Jungian archetypal psychology, the masculine or animus in women and the feminine or anima in men represent the call towards wholeness. The Lovers card of the tarot embodies the same principle: movement towards unity. Gemini strives for wholeness, bringing the inner male and female into union. The difficulty of duality is the desire to project outward what is misunderstood or unacceptable onto another. When all projections are integrated, there is no need for war outside ourselves. We no longer see things in black and white. Wholeness comes from the acceptance and understanding of our polarities. Integration comes from working with our own projections. We work with the projector, our own inner life. Unifying paradox and duality, light and dark, and destruction and creation becomes the great work. The warrior aspect of Holly can offer us the spiritual strength required to undergo this psychic journey towards wholeness.

Leda, Castor and Polydeuces' mother, was said to have been raped by a swan, but the original story depicted the swan as her trusted totem and ally. Many stories have been corrupted from their original meaning, as patriarchy established its stronghold over people's original connection to the feminine principle. In birthing children from both mortal and divine fathers, Leda created the world egg from which Castor and Pollax were born. Their polarity remained a non-combative, mutually created dynamic which contains and incubates all possibilities.

In other stories, this creation became the polarization of hostile opposites and the makings of warfare—it is a matter of perspective. Enlarging our perspective is a call towards wholeness and the evolution of human consciousness. Our higher task is to create cooperation and harmony. We can learn to focus on unity while holding the tension that is polarity. What we can't keep together must be torn asunder, and we are left with the base habit of focusing on separation, blame, and war. Love embraces opposites and cherishes differences, whereas fear kills what it views as its polar opposite. How do we stay in a state of love?

When I sing the following song, I am reminded of the inner work required to ensure the growth towards wholeness that Holly protects and encourages. I can appreciate the truly "holy" nature of this tree.

Trees, trees, trees, trees
I thank the Earth for all her trees
Alder, Cedar, Oak, and Holly
Let them all grow!
(repeat in rounds)

Guided Meditation

Holle is the goddess who represents your shadow self—all negativity is projected onto her for your benefit. She holds this energy until you are able to integrate it and claim it for yourself. We are encouraged to now give her our gratitude for her great sacrifice and service.

Close your eyes and begin with deep, cleansing breaths. Set your intention to connect with Holle and to listen and learn from her. In your mind's eye, you find yourself out at night in the spring time. It is dark and clear and although it is pleasant enough, you notice your heart beginning to feel afraid; you are aware of an icy atmosphere. You shiver.

In front of you arrives a stranger. You feel like running, but you find your intention holds you where you stand. A tall, imposing female figure approaches you holding a spear. You recognize her as Holle, the goddess of the Holly month, and remember she is the goddess of the underworld, death, and regeneration. You try to catch a glimpse of her, but realize that you have come face to face with your shadow: your own negativity and fears. Make eye contact with Holle; let her know you are here to learn. You may see your fears, judgments, and criticisms draped over her shoulder ... you recognize that she carries them for you.

Be willing to reflect on a conflict, situation, or person you are having trouble with. Or, you can choose an old pattern that keeps resurfacing. Ask Holle to show you what you need to know about yourself within the context you have presented. As you focus together, be willing to know and accept what is communicated to you without judgment or blame (on yourself or others). Take time to receive her communication … (pause)

You now notice that from Holle emanates great love and protection. She may also give you a message or a symbol to help bring your shadow into the light. Be willing to receive these from her … (pause)

When you feel you've finished your communication, offer Holle your gratitude for holding negative energy for you. She will continue to hold this kind of energy until you are ready to face your shadow again. Know that you can return to Holle anytime you desire. She offers love and support for your courage and willingness to explore your "dark side," what has been hidden. She reminds you that within any conflict or trouble, the most important responsibility is to look within and rein in your own projections. Holle reminds you that she isn't here to dredge up your inner criticisms and uncomfortable feelings; in fact, she is a tremendous ally to you. No matter who or what you find adversarial, Holle reminds you that conflict and harmony are two-way streets, and that it is easy to project outwardly your own unconsciousness: your hatred, greed, spite, and covetousness. She also reminds you that the true end to hatred and cruelty is the integration and appreciation of your own shadow.

Give your love and appreciation to Holle. When you do, you notice a great being of light entering the picture. He takes Holle's hand. There stands Lugh, the god of light. As Lugh and Holle stand together, you are able to perceive a grand whole. You realize that within their polarity is great power and consciousness. You breathe this wholeness into yourself. You feel a great sense of renewal and complete peace.

Lugh and Holle speak together: "We see your courage. We affirm your Goddess/God self. We recognize and hold your fears, weaknesses, and what you perceive as negativity within and without yourself, with compassion. From this day forward, Holle will help you to look at your projections. And Lugh will bring light to the darkness of what was hidden, denied, or outwardly projected. We form a powerful sacred marriage within your inner being. In this alchemical process, you are able to transform yourself into a being of consciousness that uplifts the world. You become a light worker, and we welcome you!"

You give your gratitude to the both of them, and feel yourself returning to this place and time. Take some deep grounding breaths and take a moment to center yourself and come fully back into your body. Journal your experiences and know that you have begun a powerful process.

Holly Healing

Plant holly trees around your house for protection from unwanted energies and people who may want to take advantage of you. Ask these trees to protect your home and your belongings. Know that Holly is your true friend and looks out for your health and welfare.

Bring Holly into the house in winter to remind you that life is always continuing, even if it is beyond the senses. Even in the dead of winter, when life seems barren and cold, life endures.

Make a wand of a holly twig or branch; keep it close to remind you to focus energies in your personal work rather than cause more difficulty in the world around you through your projections. In times of relationship strife, ask Holly to bring you into wholeness, help you understand the other person's position, and help you be a good listener.

Hazel

COLL–HAZEL

June 13–July 10
9th Lunation, June/July

Description: Hazels have large, oval leaves with toothed edges that turn yellow in autumn. They are small trees and the branches are strong and flexible. Trees bear both male and female flowers— the male are naked catkins and the female blossoms are found on separate twigs but are very small and hard to see. Nuts are called hazelnuts or filberts.

Ogham: Coll ("cull"), C: ᚉ
Insight, wisdom, intuition, higher perspective, straight to source, fulfillment, bounty, the zenith, abundance, encourages wisdom and vision, divination offers clarity, creativity

Class: Chieftain

Holiday: Summer Solstice, Alban Heruin, Midsummer, June 21

Rune: Kaunaz ᚲ
Opening, the hearth, creativity, passion, craftsmanship, instinct, bringing light to the dark, renewed clarity

Totems and Guides: Tortoise and turtles, crustaceans, salmon, scarab, Rhiannon and the hare

Astrology: Cancer, June 20/21–July 22, ♋

"I feel," a cardinal water sign of feminine polarity

Symbol: the crab

Ruling Planet: Moon ☽, the 4th house

Body Parts: Rules the breasts, stomach, and solar plexus

Colors: silver and soft shades

Keywords: mother, mothering, family, home, nurturing, emotional, protective, sensitive, fertile, evasive, changeable, moody

The Coll/Hazel Month

This summer tree month includes the celebration of the Summer Solstice on June 20 or 21, known to Celtic ancestors as Alban Heruin. Other names are Midsummer and Litha. At Midsummer, we invite the faeries to our ceremonies, as these devas and nature spirits play a central role in the organization and proliferation of plant life on our planet. We feel loving gratitude for Mother Earth. The apple tree (or Quert) shares this month with hazel. We can also bring wild rose, thyme, and heather into our ceremonies. The color for hazel is brown. This lunation is called the Mead Moon.

This month honors compassion, love, and protection. We are in tune with our feelings, and think about the past. We are protective of our friends and family. We are not afraid to cry, and are encouraged to honor the cleansing that crying brings. The astrological sign of Cancer, ruled by the moon, is a water sign that values the emotions and the home. Safety and protection are important aspects of mothering and nurturing, also Cancer themes.

The Celts honored Hazel for its wisdom. Hazel also encourages the celebration of abundance, fertility, and power. The sun is at its zenith at this time of year, and we feel deep gratitude for Earth's bounty. Call on Hazel to lead you to the source within you—ask her to facilitate the flow of your creative energy outward to where it is needed.

Hazel also encourages creativity and insight, supporting poetry, art, song, divination, and the powers of meditation. Creative energies can be used to inspire others. Hazel allows us to act as catalysts or transformers, working through the suggestions of intuition. If you find yourself blocked in a creative pursuit, call on Hazel and she will help you follow your intuition and remove blockages.

Hazel twigs and sticks have been used for divining and dowsing for water or minerals underground. It was believed that a forked hazel twig had supernatural powers. Branches were also used to make baskets, whip handles, hoops, and other similar articles. When you have to settle a dispute, take hazel branches with you, especially when dealing with property and land disputes.

Totems, Guides, and Deities

The totems of Coll/Hazel are crustaceans, the tortoise, and the salmon. We honor all shelled and protected animals: the crab, lobster, tortoise, sea turtle, and scarab beetle. These animals are lunar creatures and call to mind the watery and emotional realm; indeed, many of them begin or spend their entire lives in or around bodies of water. They teach us to set boundaries and protect what is most sensitive and vulnerable.

The scarab beetle is a symbol for the act of becoming. Recognizing the turning of a new leaf sanctifies the journey and reminds us that we can always begin again and that we are always in the process of building up and tearing down. The scarab encourages us to protect and move towards that to which we aspire. Ancient Egyptians believed people are here on Earth to rise up the ladder of their own enlightenment, helping others who aspire to do the same. In particular, emphasis was on the process of becoming.

Another symbol for Hazel is the Chariot card of the tarot, ruled by Cancer. It depicts a charioteer managing two polarized and powerful beings, usually horses, sphinxes, or other beasts of burden. The chariot's path is through the middle way, suggesting the balanced action and mediation ability of Hazel, coupled with compassionate understanding. The charioteer usually wears armor, implying protection. The persona or mask protects the more vulnerable inner being. Sometimes it's necessary to put on a brave face and allow our outward persona to protect us. Knowing we are protected helps us keep our perspective, responsiveness, and awareness without feeling exposed or endangered. The front (or shell) also offers detachment and objectivity.

The Celts believed the hazelnut encouraged vision and the buried treasure within. Coll is associated with the bardic numeral nine. In Celtic legend, nine hazelnuts fell into the fountain of wisdom and were eaten by an ordinary salmon. The salmon gained all the knowledge in the world, and was then able to shapeshift into the young maiden or into Fintan. Fintan, "the White Ancient" is the embodiment of Merlin, the magician, or the wise old man/hermit archetype. The hazel bestowed its great gifts and thus we were given the wisdom and inspiration contained in the hazelnuts.

All nuts are said to be protein-rich with precious, nutritious oils (as is salmon!), but they are also are powerful symbols of wisdom and higher perspective, encouraging the proper use of intellect.

The rabbit (sometimes known in mythology as the moon hare) is a shape-shifting magical woman who transforms into a gorgeous maiden. The Welsh goddess Rhiannon regularly shapeshifted into a rabbit, as well as a white mare. Rhiannon and the rabbit were common symbols for fertility to ancient Celts. Given the mothering qualities of the astrological sign of Cancer (ruled by the moon), we honor our female lineages. We celebrate fertility and the abundance of life in this summer month.

Guided Meditation

Close your eyes, relax, and steady your breathing. Travel internally to a safe place in nature to begin your journey. It is a warm and lovely summer day. Take time to acquaint yourself with your surroundings … (pause)

You see a dirt path leading to what seems to be a grove of trees. You follow it, and find a grove of hazel trees. Within this grove, you enter into the energy field of your ancestral clan mothers. You begin to feel a strong sense of respect for the women in your lineages.

The DNA of the divine feminine ancestor is honored in this special, sacred place, and you feel welcomed. Here, female wisdom is considered holy. You are reminded that every woman carries within her the genetic code that marked the evolution of the first woman, and that all evolutional changes have been passed down through this female line. You remember that in ancient times, sovereignty and royal blood was originally only traced through the mother and that kingship was conferred through marriage to the queen. The royal blood of the Goddess, the divine ancestress, was passed from mother to daughter. With her many names, the Goddess protects and nurtures our genetic memory of wisdom, maternal protection, and resurrection. She is the human clan mother and you are her child. She has watched you grow up and mature.

The awesome, powerful clan mother steps out of the grove and makes herself known. She is the priestess of Hazel, and embodies the love of the great mother, wisdom, and protection. Notice how she is dressed, and observe her demeanor. She beckons you forward with a loving gesture. Walk to her. Your eyes meet, and she looks at you with intense love and understanding. Take in her beauty and power, and feel her joy and acceptance.

Notice that behind her, your female relatives begin to show up. Your mother and her female lineage begin to congregate, and the women from your father's side of the family join the group. Standing with you are your sisters and daughters. Be aware of your own mother, her mother behind her, and so on, stretching toward the infinite horizon. Give recognition to your father's mother, her mother behind her, and all the way back to the infinite horizon as well. Feel the powerful womanly connection flowing to you and forward into your daughters, sisters, nieces, granddaughters, and friends. Feel the love here and the compassion; here there is nothing but eager interest and enthusiasm. Messages you need to hear will be given to you in loving support of your efforts, struggles, creativity, and desires. If you have any special needs or desires, share them. If you have any questions, ask them at this time. The mothers of your lines want your fulfillment and are willing to lend energy and support. Listen to the gentle messages of your feminine lineages ... (long pause) When you feel ready, give your gratitude and watch these loving women return to other dimensions.

The priestess of Hazel steps forward and kisses you on either cheek. She hands you something, calling it a "crane bag." In here, she says, you are to place that which represents your special, personal medicine. It can contain stories, poems, songs, dances, art, rituals, incantations, blessings, divinations, symbols, history, and anything else of personal significance. Take a moment to visualize the crane bag and think about what you will place in it. As you imagine these things, they magically appear. If you conjure large items, don't worry—when you place them into your bag, they will change in size to fit. This crane bag is a symbol of yourself: you are the wisdom and magic. It is protection, guidance, connection, and an honoring of your DNA. Take your time as you gather what you want to place into the bag ... (pause)

After filling your crane bag, you sense it is time to stand up and give your gratitude to the priestess. Also thank the hazel grove that has supported the connection to the women of your lineage and the honor of being born a woman in this lifetime. Take a moment to remember messages from your lineages and the love of the Goddess, and to review what you placed in your crane bag. When you are ready, you may return to this time and place and record your journey in your journal.

You may want to purchase or make a little bag and gather some special things to represent what you imagined in this journey. This is your personal good medicine pouch, and will remind you of your connection to all clan mothers.

Hazel Tree Healing

Eat some hazelnuts when you are seeking wisdom and a higher perspective. Spend time by a wild stream and watch for fish, crabs, and river life. Tune in to the wisdom that is offered. If you can't physically be in nature, visit in your mind's eye.

When you face a difficult decision, seek Hazel's guidance. She will inform you with her powerful knowledge and wisdom. Seek communication directly with Merlin or Thoth, embodiments of truth, wisdom, and communication. They will direct you to the right books, teachers, and helpers. Coll/Hazel with help you overcome any creative blocks. She will help you follow your intuitive path, rather than a logically conceived, analytical plan. Hazel offers inspiration, creativity, and inner guidance.

Hazel sticks are excellent for divining due to their pliancy. Dowsing rods can be used to find underground water, precious metals, or even lost objects. Rods of hazel can be used for making fences, fishing rods, and hoops.

Apple

QUERT–APPLE
Shares with the Coll/Hazel Month

Description: Apple trees belong to the rose family. They can grow to be quite large. Beautiful blossoms develop in the spring and the namesake fruit appears in late summer and fall. There are many small leaves on individual stems.

Ogham: Quert ("kwert"), Q: ≣
Choice and beauty. This tree shares the month with the Coll Hazel and is a dual tree for the months of July and August. It also represents the Goddess, connection to the female lineage and to one's home or ancestral land, Gaia, and Mother Earth.

Class: Shrub

Rune: Perth ⟨ᚲ⟩
Initiation, something hidden, a secret matter. This is a mystery rune and suggests powerful forces of change are at play. Expect surprises. Seek higher perspective. External events and situations exist only to show you an inner reflection. Renewal of the spirit is promised. The phoenix rises from its ashes to begin anew, becoming whole.

Totems: apples, faeries and little people, the pentacle, all goddesses in their many names and many forms, ancestors, female lineages, the land of your ancestry, Glastonbury, the Apple Isle, Gaia, Mother Earth, nature

Astrology: Cancer (see page 118)

The Quert/Apple Month

The Apple is regarded as a sacred, magical tree, symbolizing fruitfulness and fulfillment. Apples themselves have long been symbols of nature's harvest and abundance. Within the fruit is the pentagram, symbolic of the earth element and the bounty of Gaia, our Mother Earth. The apple is also a symbol of the magical isle of Avalon and is connected to beauty, magic, and the ancient European worship of the Goddess. The apple tree also represents having to make a choice between good things, or a decision-making time in a person's life. The apple tree's color is green.

Druids favored the apple tree, as it hosted one of their sacred plants, the mistletoe, and grew near oak groves, also important to them. Everywhere around the world, the apple is seen as a sacred, magical, and holy fruit. It is a symbol for fertility and immortality.

The fruit of this tree has long been thought to be a panacea, and many cures, myths, and legends call for its use.

Paris gave Aphrodite an apple to show that she was the most beautiful of all of the goddesses. Apples are given to teachers as a gift of special recognition, and we've all heard the expression "an apple a day keeps the doctor away."

The apple represents abundance in your life, and your blessings. Apple reminds us to be grateful for what we have, so that the universe can continue to send its goodness to us.

The ogham, quert, is a mandate to rest and heal yourself from strife, illness, fatigue, or injury. You are invited to regain a sense of wholeness and reconnect with nature. Apple stands as your loving mother, prepared to support you with unconditional love and acceptance.

Totems, Guides, and Deities

Anicent Greeks believed there was an isle in the western ocean where golden apples of the Hesperides (the nymphs who guarded these golden apples) could be found. Eating one was said to bestow immortality.

Legends of King Arthur describe a special island called Avalon, or "the Isle of Apples," a paradise and sanctuary of the Goddess, eventually enveloped in the mist as Britain turned from the early Goddess spirituality, and embraced Christianity. We are reminded of a special dimension of reality in which magic is the norm. (Read Marion Zimmer Bradley's *Mists of Avalon* to reconnect with the mystery and magic of ancient goddess worship in the British Isles.)

Many goddesses around the world are associated with the apple as it relates to fertility and motherhood. Apple-related goddesses were responsible for healings, the gift of love, and abundance. Avalon was ruled by the Faerie Queen, Morgan le Fay, and her priestesses. It is said that Merlin received the gift of prophecy after consuming apples given by Morgan herself within a sacred grove guarded by birds. Another apple-goddess figure is the Lady of the Lake, who taught the Welsh physicians of Myddfai their healing arts. These physicians passed down their knowledge of plant medicine through time.

The quest for wisdom in Ireland was symbolized in the pursuit of the white doe under a wild apple tree. It was believed that silver boughs cut from magical apple trees produced silver apple-shaped bells that played a mystical tune. Shaking the musical branch could be used to lull people into trance states that allowed them to travel between the worlds.

Guided Meditation

You find yourself in a lovely apple orchard, a beautiful place that embraces the fullness of summer. The season's abundance is all around you, and you smile as you reach for a juicy, red apple hanging from a tree close by. As you bite into the sweetness, you find yourself transported to the Isle of Avalon. You immediately know you have entered a magic domain, but you also understand that you are completely safe and protected.

Walking around, what you most notice here is a sense of beauty and contentment—you enjoy being here very much. Everything seems to be in harmony and balance and you feel honored to be allowed to visit here. You understand that this is a dimension that honors the Goddess and the Earth. You notice animals shyly coming closer to you: a doe and her fawn, rabbits, and small birds. The sounds of crickets, frogs, and the sweet twitters of birds surround you. There are trees of all kinds in this place, but you focus on a beautifully sculpted apple tree with round, red fruit.

You feel a need to pick one of the apples, but you don't know which one. Each apple appears to represent a different choice, yet each choice is something you desire. Take a moment to look at the different choices in your life right now. One may be to change residences, another may be to travel, another may be to take the next step closer to a commitment in your relationship, a new job, a money opportunity, a new project or enterprise, time spent alone, or whatever you want. Take time to consider your choices ... (pause)

When the time feels right, choose one and hold it close to your heart. If you see a symbol on the apple's skin, focus on it, for this will represent your choice. Take the apple into your being and allow it to fill you with resolve and potential. You have all the energy you will need to embrace this choice, and you know you can return to this tree to make other choices at other times. In the choice of this one delicious apple, you will enjoy its sweetness completely!

It is time to give gratitude to this magical place and to this very special apple tree. This is your tree—full of adventure, potential, and opportunities. Gently return to this place and time. Open your eyes when you are ready, and be sure to ground and center. Record your journey in your journal, taking note of the special symbol on the apple you chose. Write about that apple, and think about ways you can nurture, protect, and move forward into manifestation.

Apple Tree Healing

Apple will take your heartache and return the energy to the earth to be transmuted; the same thing she did for me in my apple tree story. She will help purify and heal the wounds of the heart. Apple serves as a great loving mother, and will fill you with life-force energy and renewed hope. She holds sacred ground for you in a way that no human can. Any energy you can no longer carry can be handled by Apple with ease. She absorbs that negative energy and sends it back into the earth through her root systems for the highest good and transformation. In her energy transfer, we are reminded that everything is without labels, beyond concepts of "good" and "bad." Any negative or hurtful energy can be transformed to another, more beneficial form.

When you suffer from bitterness, irritation, or anger, or if you suffer from a feeling of worthlessness, Apple can help modify and soothe these emotions. She can help you remove blocks in the flow of your body's life-force energy so you can open up to the flow and abundance of the universe.

Apple helps clear feelings of shame and remorse. Her message is one of self-forgiveness. She builds a renewed sense of self-worth and self-love.

Baking an apple dessert can make you feel nostalgic, or more at home. Bringing her fragrance and taste into your home warms up your life and brings sweetness to your family.

Sitting underneath an apple tree can bring renewal back into your awareness. Apple will assist you when you want to enter a trance state and make contact with the other realms. She assists in the transformation process that occurs during guided imagery or journeying.

Apple can also represent the spiritual warrior, fearless when traveling beyond the mortal realm to face death, sacrifice, and hardship in order to benefit her people. The energy of apple helps shelter and protect you on intense shamanic journeys. If you have a loved one in the military, on a medical response team, or in public security, send them the protective energies of Apple.

As a fruit, apples are full of vitamins and minerals. They strengthen your metabolism, balance digestion, stimulate blood-cell production, and cleanse the system. They have been prescribed for intestinal infections, constipation, mental and physical fatigue, hypertension, rheumatism, gout, anemia, bronchitis, urine retention, hepatic disorders, gastric and kidney malfunctions, hoarseness, coughing, and excess cholesterol in the blood. Perhaps it was their myraid medical applications that led to their importance as fruits of knowledge and immortality.

MUIN–VINE

July 11–August 7
10th Lunation, July/beginning of August

Description: All vines and brambles are considered important to this month. Blackberry bushes and grape vines give us the fruit we so enjoy. The grape grows on a woody vine with three-pronged wide leaves. These vines usually require some kind of support to grow.

Ogham: Muin ("muhn"), M: ᚋ
Harvest, fruits of one's labor, prophecy, the clan or community, the results of the sacred marriage, gratitude and celebration

Class: Chieftain

Holiday: Lammas, August 1, Day of the Bread, a celebration to express gratitude for the first harvest and the fulfillment of summer

Rune: Mannaz ᛗ
The Self. Avoid hubris and choose humility. To thine own self be true. Know thyself. Representing the power of the sun (sons) and their procreating abilities.

Totems and Guides: Lion, Dionysus, the Green Man, Pan, sylphs, nymphs, elves and fairies, the sun god Lugh, Strength card of the tarot, Sekhmet, Kuan Yin, all mother aspect of the goddess

Vine

Astrology: Leo, July 22–August 22, ♌
   "I will," a fixed fire sign of male polarity
Symbol: lion
Ruling Planet: Sun ☉, the 5th house
Body Parts: Rules the heart and spine
Colors: gold and scarlet
Keywords: power, leadership, generosity, enthusiastic, creative, dramatic, heart full, proud, regal, arrogant

The Muin/Vine Month

The cross-quarter celebration that falls during this month is Lammas, on August 1. Lammas celebrates the beginning of the harvest and is often called the celebration of the bread. *In vino veritas* refers to the release of truth-telling and prophetic powers through the grape and effects of wine. Psychic sense is released, and your deepest emotions can come forward. Gather together all signs and omens to allow yourself to comprehend the truth. The color for vine is variegation, or multiple colors as they appear in a leaf. This lunation is called the Wort Moon, referring to a beer or whiskey made from malt and water.

Vine heralds the fulfillment of summer. Wine brings altered states of consciousness, ecstasy, visions, and divine madness. Dionysus and the Celtic Green Man are associated with Vine, as is Pan and his host of sylphs, nymphs, and faeries. In order to capture the mood of this month, recall the delightful confusion between the mortals and faeries in Shakespeare's *A Midsummer Night's Dream*.

Harvest time brings feelings of gregariousness, frivolity, and generosity. It is a time for social expansiveness—imbibing of the grape was a social collective endeavor. The harvest period falls under the astrological sign of Leo, ruled by the sun. Abundance, self-expression, and generosity of the heart all apply in this jovial time. Rituals of this period are for gratitude and fulfillment. Songs, praises, storytelling, theatrics, musical performances, and even bawdy tales are all encouraged. Leo is the sign of royalty, and at this time, we honor our progeny, the fruit of our own human vine. Although the lower vibration of Leo can encourage pride and arrogance, the higher vibration unites creativity and heart, and encourages generosity, leadership, and abundance.

Totems, Guides, and Deities

The Vine month honors the aspect of the goddess as mother. In Ireland, she is called Danu, the root word *dan* meaning knowledge. Her people were known as the *Tuatha dé Dannan*, the people of the goddess Danu. In the Welsh tradition, *Modron* ("great mother") is honored as the mother of *Mabon* ("bright son"). Another Welsh mother goddess was Don, the mother of several deities. The goddess Brigit is viewed as both a virgin and a mother, much like Arianrhod (one of Don's children). Though she was also a war goddess, Macha of the triple-aspect Morrigan was considered a mother goddess, as was Maeve. These mother goddesses were known for their holy wells, fertility, protection, and nurturance, as well as their ability to heal. Ancient Egypt's Hathor was a goddess of motherhood, ecstasy, and bliss. She encouraged people to lose themselves in dance and song and the wild beat of the drum.

Holy union of the stag/god/hunter with these great queens of the realm ensured the next year's sprouting of the seeds at Beltane. The fulfillment of their union resulted in pregnancy and the birth of their special child in December.

The priestesses of Dionysus were known as the Maenads (Bacchantes to the Romans). They were often portrayed as a frenzied retinue, becoming mad and ecstatically wild from drinking wine and dancing, but they were also his nurses when he was growing up. Tammuz, Dumuzi, Modron, and Adonis are all such sons—specially born of the Earth Mother.

These unique children were the literal fruit of the womb of the earth. They represented the crops that were reaped every summer for the good of the community. Please note that in no context are we discussing human sacrifice! Rituals performed were symbolic dramatizations. Although animals were sometimes sacrificed, the original substance used was menstrual blood, thought to be very pure and powerful. The idea of the sacrament of the last supper of Christ was originally a Dionysian ritual wherein women ate a piece of bread shaped like him (representing his body) and drank wine (his blood). Through this ritualized consumption, the women took in and absorbed the wild, potent power of nature.

The ancient Greeks used tools resembling T-squares to cultivate grapevines. Later, these Tau cross tools morphed into the structure adopted by the Romans for crucifixion. It is important to note that the story of Jesus of Nazareth is not a new one; long before Jesus, stories of sacrifice, death, and rebirth existed. The story's running theme is the ending of one yearly cycle and the death and rebirth of the sun and its seasons.

The tarot card related to this month is Strength. The fearsome lion is befriended through gentle persuasion and becomes a compassionate ally. This animal is also Vine's totem, symbolizing the sun and personal will and purpose. The lion represents the element of fire and is linked to our third chakra—the solar plexus—the center of our will.

As a totem, the lioness is royal, loving, and benevolent. She exudes heat and light, and offers assimilation. She represents the energies of the will, and she encourages us to elevate this active energy to the heart center, which offers compassion, relationship, and awareness.

The Egyptian goddess Sekhmet is another lion-related ally and was known as a fierce protector. She can be as gentle as a domesticated cat (represented in the goddess Bast), or she can become a ferocious predator. She also represents the calming and all-loving compassion seen in a goddess like Kuan Yin. Sekhmet is a staunch sentinel along your spiritual path, and she will let you know when you stray. When treated with attention, gentleness, respect, and a proper attitude, she will provide loyal service.

Guided Meditation

Sit quietly for a moment and breathe deeply. Turn your attention to your heart and draw energy from above and below into your heart, exhaling it in all directions. With every exhalation, release any current tension and concerns. As you inhale, fill yourself with the invigorating energy offered from above and below. Close your eyes and enjoy a few moments of silence.

The Vine month honors the mother aspect of the goddess in her fullness. The sun is at its zenith, and we celebrate abundance. This marks the time of year when we celebrate our blessings, happiness, and wealth. We are open to ecstasy, intoxication, and bliss.

In your mind's eye, envision yourself on a hill. From your vantage point, you can see fertile fields in the valley below, their stalks of wheat and corn appearing as a moving, golden lake. You also see fertile orchards, trees heavy with ripening fruit, and vines bursting with grapes and berries. In the hot summer sun, you take a moment to inhale this incredible bounty from Mother Earth, feeling grateful and blessed. All around, you see beautiful opened flowers, full of scent and color.

Suddenly, you are interrupted by an approaching group of people making music, singing, and laughing. At the front of the group is an attractive and vibrant young man who you guess is the leader. He is wearing a crown of vine and is accompanied by a group of women you know as the Maenads. You realize this man is Dionysus, Lord of the Vine. Also in the group you spot a figure who appears to be half-man and half-goat, much to your amazement. You recognize him as Pan, god of the wild and the pastures. A beautiful Mother Goddess approaches you and takes your hand, and the whole group skips and laughs as you follow a path to what looks to be a sacred grove. She lets you know that you are here today to celebrate her bounty and that she is glad that you responded to her call.

The dancing and merriment begins as you enter the grove. You find yourself with a lovely glass of wine, mead, or grape juice (if you prefer) and before you stands a long table laid with an abundance of fruits, vegetables, and breads. The grove is filled with all kinds of magical beings, and you begin to dance and frolic. The laughter and merriment is almost unbearable, but you lose yourself to the joy and ecstasy of the celebration. The music and song is divine. Allow your imagination to embrace this moment, and feel whisked away. Sometimes you dance with the Goddess, then with Dionysus, then with Pan, a Maenad, and with the fairy folk. You turn from one wonderful partner to another in wild abandon and merriment. The drums become faster and the music rises to a feverish pitch. You dance faster and faster and surrender yourself to pure bliss ... (pause)

All of a sudden, the music stops and the crowd moves to form a large circle. Each participant takes a turn, giving gratitude for this time of year and something he or she is personally grateful for. When it comes to your turn, make sure you thank this gathering for including you, and then share what you are grateful for this year. When everyone has spoken, each group member comes to you with a smile and shares a word of encouragement. Dionysus stands in front of you; listen to his words. Then Pan; listen to his words, then the Maenads, the nymphs of the forest and the vine, and finally the Mother Goddess in whatever form you see her. Listen carefully to their words of encouragement and wisdom ... (long pause)

When you are finished, say your goodbyes and prepare to return to this time and space. Gently come back to your body, and ground and center yourself. As soon as you feel able, write your experiences in your journal. What were the messages shared with you, and what were you especially grateful for?

Vine Healing

Vine is helpful when you are trying to become pregnant. Call in her power and make time to create a special ceremony before you have sexual intercourse. Think of the sexual act as the sacred union between the Horned God and the Mother Goddess. Call on Vine immediately before or after giving birth; Vine carries the sun's energy of vigor and strength. Use vine when you are giving a ceremony to welcome a newborn to increase the bounty and good luck for the child.

Use Vine when you wish to give thanks for your "children." Celebrate what you have given birth to, and honor the fruits of your labor. This can be your actual children, or projects, activities, and plans. Likewise, when you need a burst of creative energy for a new project, or when you want to see one to its completion, call on Vine.

Vine may also be summoned when you are healing or asking for healing, or in matters related to divination and prophecy.

When you do your August gardening, be aware of the magic of the fruits. Reflect on the miracle of growth—the fruits, vegetables, and grains planted with loving care earlier in the year. Hold blessing ceremonies in which you give gratitude for the harvest of growing crops in the fields, and on the plants, vines, and trees. Have a party and enjoy yourself!

Hold a women's circle of family members to share the stories of your mothers, grandmothers, and great-grandmothers. When I presented heirlooms and paintings to my nieces, we sat in circle and I shared stories I knew about the women in my family. In this way, I ensured that the stories and sentimental objects in my family were being passed along. I also shared experiences I'd had with these relatives through dreams, communications, and synchronicities.

Have a "boasting" party. We are all taught to not get too full of ourselves or be self-centered. As a result, it seems we often hide our light from others and fail to take our moments in the sun. We all need applause and recognition, and it is a wonderful experience to open up to praise and encouragement. In a boasting party, each woman gets a designated period of time to boast about herself. When she is finished, everyone gives her their applause. In this way, we can claim our right to feel proud and can talk about our accomplishments. Vine encourages each of us to be our own star.

If I had to guess what the one form of currency for entering other realms would be, I would say gratitude. Keep a gratitude journal and write down something you are grateful for every day. This small practice can change your life. The unseen realms hear you and appreciate the attention. They are more than willing to respond and enrich your life when you express your happiness and gratefulness.

Share what you have with others. This time of year encourages abundance and generosity. Give your resources, money, and time. Pick a charity or an important cause to support.

Call on Sekhmet in times of mental weakness; she is a very powerful ally to have. She has helped me many times when I forget that I *do* have a backbone. She gives me strength and the occasional good kick in the butt as a wake-up for when I'm not being my own best advocate. She has provided me with courage and unconditional love. Read more about her and ask her if she will work with you. She is one of the best protectors and always has your best interests at heart.

Ivy

GORT – IVY

August 8–September 4
11th Lunation, August/early September

Description: Ivy loves to climb up trees, around poles, and on fences. Her leaves have three prongs and are often variegated in color. Ivy loves to grow in spirals, up and around things.

Ogham: Gort ("gor' it"), G:
The labyrinth into the center of ourselves, our inner knowing, the spiral into our own souls

Class: Chieftain

Rune: Gebo ⊠
The partnership rune, freedom, separateness and union, harmony, the giving of gifts, hospitality, contracts, agreements, sexuality, a union with the Higher Self

Totems and Guides: Spider, Wolf, Anubis, Spider Woman, Arachne, the three Fates, the Weaver as guardian of our fate

Astrology: Arachne (no symbol)
Evidence suggests there was once a zodiac of thirteen signs, each twenty-eight days in duration. One was dropped at one point, that of Arachne, the spider. It may be that Virgo was once two signs, Hera-Athena and Arachne, represented by Vine and Ivy. Arachne is

the mighty aspect of the great mother as the spinner and creator of the physical world. Within the existing twelve-sign zodiac, the Gort/Ivy month includes the energies of Leo (ending on August 22) and Virgo (beginning on August 23).

The Gort/Ivy Month

Ivy grows in even the harshest of environments, always reaching for the light. We can emulate ivy's behavior to develop and refine ourselves: she represents the spiral into ourselves and the search for the center. She represents the journey of inner discovery and connection. The color for Gort is *gorm*, sky blue. This lunation is called the Barley Moon.

In the Greek myth, Theseus led himself out of the labyrinth using a ball of twine given to him by the princess Ariadne, after his encounter with the Minotaur (his shadow). Likewise, as we travel through our lives, we find that we must circle back to ourselves. How have we changed? What changes can we now anticipate?

Ivy is similar to Holly in that it represents life force. Ivy grows in spirals, representing evolutionary growth, resurrection, and the continual return of life, renewal even after devastation. Ivy plays a feminine balance to Holly. While Holly is the staff, club, or spear, Ivy is the encircling energy of rebirth and growth. Together, these represent the cycles of life.

Ivy promises triumph; she can grow roots anywhere and can bring green life back. She offers understanding of the return to the self, that inward journey into our core and heart. At the center, we merge with the universal life force.

For the next three months, the cup will be our alchemical focus. The cup (or chalice) holds the depths of our emotion and love and offers an elixir to aid us in creating the life we know is possible. Opposite the feminine nature of the chalice is the blade. We can cut away what is not needed, and reap what we have sown and nurtured through the year. As we grow towards the light, like the green ivy, we can use intellect (the blade) and compassion (the chalice) to create more satisfying experiences and to take command of our lives through the direction and guidance of spirit. The connection to inner guidance is found within.

Totems, Guides, and Deities

Arachne the spider and the Wolf are Ivy's totems. The spider is a totem of the Goddess as a weaver of destiny. She is a creative force as she threads, creates, and encloses. Spider is the symbol of our connectedness, the strands of her web transferring vibration between us all, a reminder that everything we do affects others. We are all connected through Spider.

Spider is forever creating and expanding, yet when frustrated, she can turn against herself and become self-destructive. Of similar nature is the scorpion, stinging itself. When we become too internal and self-critical, our own self-loathing and hatred can be destructive in the same way. We must take care and help each other remain hopeful, creative, and expansive.

As a goddess, Spider appears in the Native American Spider Woman, the Tibetan Iktomi, and the ancient Egyptian Grandmother Neith, the weaver. Spider creates patterns of energy in her universal loom. Her web symbolizes the warp and weave of all possibilities. It is through her weaving that potentialities are made manifest. What is it we wish to manifest? Can we become more conscious of what we create and recognize our responsibility in this process?

The theme of weaving and creating extends to the creation of the self. Here we unite our personalities with the greater forces of love and compassion. Our lives are woven from the choices we make and the feelings and thoughts we create. As embodied in goddess form, weavers provide insight, knowledge, unconditional love, and courage towards achieving our personal best. When infused with the power of spirit, we can do more healing than we ever thought possible.

Spirals, the labyrinth, the structure of DNA, the helix, and the ca-
duceus are all forms close to Ivy. The labyrinth is a symbol for the
path that leads to our core. As you walk a labyrinth, you circle around
and around to finally meet yourself at the center, where we find the
entire universe. The labyrinth is a sacred spiral symbol creating a sacred dance and motion. We go to the core, our own inner place, and
meet the mystery.

At the center, you might also meet your shadow. Here, Wolf will
be your ally—he will protect and guard you as you explore your own
inner fears and the negative things you judge about yourself. He is
your loyal guide in the underworld and can take you safely into yourself through intuition, dreams, vision, and memories. He can make
you aware of the thought-forms and emotional patterns that no longer serve you. He can help you understand and heal your pain. With
his help, you can safely enter and navigate the realms of the unconscious or lower self.

Wolf can approach and introduce you to the great goddesses and
gods who represent primary energy. Wolf can also handle any negative inner archetype or demon you may encounter upon your inner
journey.

Painful or uncomfortable times are important opportunities for
the active transformation of ideologies and concepts, habits, judgments, behavior patterns, and emotional limitations. In order to
re-create our existence at a higher level, each of us at times, must
journey alone. That is, only you can accurately reflect on your life.
Personal work must be done alone, allowing that which no longer
serves to be alchemized so that the new may be created.

Wolves mate for life and teach us about relationships and community. They live in packs, and play and hunt together. They are intelligent and family-oriented. Though wolf society has a hierarchy, it is
not rigid, and no wolf's role is more important than another. Many
people think being the alpha (leader) wolf is the best position, but al-
phas rarely live to old age and are constantly threatened by potential
usurpers.

Another ally is the Egyptian god Anubis, the jackal-headed one. While he oversees the practice of embalming, he is also a wonderful guide, offering his service if you but ask. He is a loyal protector as the guardian of abandoned children and helps us navigate through threshold experiences. As the opener of the way, he will help you through death and rebirth experiences.

Guided Meditation

In your mind's eye, travel to a favorite location. Take time to familiarize yourself within this place. Notice the time of day, the weather, and the general atmosphere. When you are acclimated, invoke the priestess of Ivy. After a moment, she appears in a green cloak and crown of ivy. Her red hair brightly contrasts with the dark green of her clothing. She approaches and greets you with warmth and affection. In this moment, make eye contact with her and give her your gratitude for coming to meet with you. Ask her to assist and guide you in your spiraled travel into yourself.

Next, envision a labyrinth. You stand at the entrance. The priestess hands you a ball of twine and holds the loose end. She nods at you and smiles, reassuring you that she will stand as your guard, holding the thread firmly. You enter the labyrinth and gently unroll the ball.

Though it is dark and very quiet inside, you feel perfectly safe. Take time to get your bearings, all the while unraveling the ball of twine … (pause) Finally, you reach the center. Here you encounter a manifestation of the weaver. She may appear as a spider, Spider Woman, the Egyptian goddesses Neith, Isis, or Maat (the goddess of justice and order), or she may appear as a fairy godmother or medicine woman. All are aspects of the mothers of our fate—our genetic code and rebirths.

Greet the weaver and give her your gratitude. Allow yourself to receive any information about your life's purpose and your current path she might have to share with you. Be open in your communication, and if you need strength or realignment, ask for it and be specific. You may ask the weaver questions, but be patient—sometimes answers come later ... (pause)

When you feel the experience is nearing completion, be sure to give gratitude to your helper once again. Thank your manifestation of the weaver for her communication, energetic healing, and support. Know that you can return to this place and guide anytime you want.

The weaver recedes into the darkness, and you sense it is time to follow your string out of the labyrinth and return to the priestess ... (pause) You wind your way back to the entrance and see her standing exactly where you left her. She seems very happy to see you, and showers you with love. Be willing to receive her blessings. Share with her what you learned and ask her if she has any further communication or energetic transmission for you ... (pause) Return her ball of twine, expressing thankfulness, and indicate you must depart.

Begin to return to this time and space, and your body. Slowly open your eyes, ground, and center yourself. When you feel ready, record your experiences in your journal. What form did the weaver take for you? What was said about your purpose and your current path? What questions did you ask? What messages were given? Did you receive a sense of renewed strength and realignment?

Ivy Healing

When your feelings and memories spiral around to an old wound, ask Ivy to strengthen your resolve to handle it in a loving way, free of shame and regret. Although the pain and upset may feel intense, hold it close without becoming destructive. Visualize holding the uncomfortable pressure within your cauldron. As these wounds tend to show up again, we can continue reaching for the light as we ascend. What is the lesson? What are you learning? Ivy instructs you through example, ever growing upwards. Ivy assures you that you will do the same. When you revisit painful experiences or memories, Ivy gently reminds you that you are only revisiting this place, not experiencing it for the first time. Soon, the intensity will pass as you grow upward in your own spiral.

Spider can help to reweave a new pattern of wholeness for any situation. Wolf can assure you protection and lead you down the path of your inner good, no matter what happens. Seek your own good and take time in determining your plan of action (or inaction). Send love to all and let the universe do its work. Send love to your problems through the Goddess—she knows how to love everything and everyone. After you've treated your problems and past failings with respect and love, let them go … they will be resolved.

Do some weaving to connect yourself to the weaving goddesses. You don't have to have a complicated loom; weaving can be done on something as simple as a cardboard square. Take care in selecting your materials; you can choose ribbon, thread, yarn, embroidery floss, or whatever you want. Give each string in your weaving a name. One could be love, another hope, another strength, and so on. Your cross strands could be named fun, abundance, flexibility, humor, joy, and so on. As you create your piece (your peace), fully identify with the process of creation. Sense how your life is created. Do you choose beauty, hope, fun, and encouragement, or do you gather strands of anger, judgment, despair, and skepticism?

When you need courage, imagine a strong ivy plant growing towards the light. Remember that no matter how dark it gets, we always strive for the light. Ivy can grow through tiny cracks and crevices, and is incredibly hardy. You hold the same pattern within yourself. Buy a little ivy plant to help remind you of this when you are going through challenging times.

If you find yourself too overextended and need some retreat time, call on Ivy. She will nudge you back into your own center and sight. She will help you to receive nourishment from within before you move outwardly again.

If you ever decide to seek professional psychological therapy, ask the totems, guides, and deities of Ivy to be present in your process. They will help light the way for you and hold you in sacred space. They will give you the courage and safety you require.

NGETAL~REED

September 5—October 2
12th Lunation, September

Description: Reeds include grasses, pampas grass, bamboo, cattails, and any plant with long, hollow shoots.

Ogham: Ngetal ("nyettle," "ing-tal"), ng:
Direct action

Class: Shrub

Rune: Ingwaz
The field of all potentials and possibility, intention, fertility, completion, resolution, yielding to a greater power, invoking the mystery, movement

Holiday: September 20 or 21, Autumn Equinox, Mabon, Alban Elved

Totems and Guides: Owl and Pike, Athena, Artemis, Hecate, Lilith, Cerdiwen, the Crone, DNA's double helix

Astrology: Virgo, August 22–September 22, ♍
    "I analyze," a mutable earth sign of feminine polarity
Symbol: a virginal maiden
Ruling Planet: Mercury ☿, the 6th house
Body Parts: Rules the intestinal tract and powers of assimilation
Colors: gray and navy blue

Reed

Keywords: discriminating, analytical, critical, health, service, methodical, details, work ethic, healing, problem solving, healing practices

The Ngetal/Reed Month

The Reed month includes the celebration of the autumnal equinox (Alban Elved, or Mabon), falling on September 20 or 21. The holiday occurs when the sun enters Libra in late September. Day and night are equal, and there is balance and harmony of lunar and solar energies. From this day forward, hours of darkness will exceed the number of hours of daylight until the vernal equinox. This time is wonderful for rituals of inner balancing.

Mabon is a harvest festival and a preparatory period for winter's coming darkness. If you have an altar, decorate it with fruits of the harvest like nuts, small pumpkins, squashes, and fall leaves. Call in the goddesses of the harvest: Demeter, Corn Mother, Ker, and Ceres. Call the Egyptian vulture goddess Nekhbet for balance and judgment, and Hecate to break down and make useful the leftover debris from reaping, harvesting, and cutting away. The name Mabon is another name for the equinox which honors Queen Mab of the faeries. I love to give gratitude and appreciation for all the unseen help the little people and nature's devas or spirits provide—they support the cycles of growth for the plant life that sustains us. This period falls under the sign of Virgo, a mutable earth sign. This lunation is called the Wine Moon.

Reed calls for direct action, accuracy, and focused aim toward the center (bull's eye) of what you desire. This is a threshold month in which you can set and deliver your last intentions for the year's ending—everything you've worked for requires only direction and intent to be brought to fruition. Reed is like a well-aimed arrow, and the bow is your energy and emotion, directing your intention. Speaking your intention out loud contributes to this process. If you like, ask someone to witness you speaking your intention.

Reeds have long, slender shafts, reminiscent of pea shooters or flutes. Whether these are used as weapons or instruments, they require the use of the breath. We breathe life into our intentions. There is a related saying that we should be a "hollow bone," as exemplified in the structures of hollow reeds, bullrushes, bamboo, and pampas grasses. What it means is that we can deliberately allow spirits to work through us by directing our intention, in effect becoming co-creators. We must be willing to let go of whatever impedes this process. As we move towards winter, we can cut away that which no longer serves our greater purposes. We look to dispose of harmful, negative, and destructive habits on the way to our becoming whole.

Watching, waiting, and precisely striking our target is the blueprint for manifesting what we desire. Reed reminds us that everything in our world is improved when we work towards manifesting our aspirations with spirit. When our hopes and dreams include helping others, spirit provides us an extra boost of energy.

We are reminded of stories where precious children were hidden in the reeds from danger, and then found and rescued by their foster mothers. It is a theme in many stories throughout history: Moses, Heracles, Perseus, Oedipus, Jason, and Anubis all share this commonality. Reed offers protection until just the right moment, and then the godmother appears, gathering us up and protecting us. The meaning can extend to our projects and dreams. Protect them until just the right time, and be ready to release your intent for their growth and nurturing into the world.

Have you ever noticed that over-talking your ideas before you start something actually dissipates the energy? There is a period when creations must be protected, nurtured, and held close to the heart. Think of this period as being "in the reeds." Then, when the time is right, ask some very close and trusted friend whom you do not find jealous or overly critical of you to act as your fairy godmother. This person will help you to get your "baby" out there into the world. The person might be your editor, your agent, or your secretary. Or you yourself may have to take on the role. Make a plan—with the fairy-godmother person (or yourself), determine what you need to do to get your work or project out there, or ask the person to help you strategize different steps.

When everything is in place and you are ready to send your intention out into the world, it's very helpful to write "treatments" for your goals. An example would be, "I am so grateful for the success of my class. I have more than enough students and ample salary. I am thrilled with my students' efforts and joy, and I am excited that I can teach them well. I give my gratitude to the universe and know this is already mine. I accept my good and so it is." From that point on, go about doing things on a daily basis to forward your plans. Your godmother will help you. Refrain from placing any negativity into your expectations and keep your intention clear. If you fill your treatment statements with "I sure hope this doesn't happen" or "I don't want such-and-such for students" or "I don't want this-and-that," the universe doesn't feel your positivity, and has a harder time sending it to you. It is best to release your good, positively formed intentions into the universe and know the outcome is already yours. This way, you'll shoot your arrow into the air, aimed with joy and complete understanding of how manifestation happens.

Totems, Guides, and Deities

Owl and Pike are the totems of Reed. Both these animals hunt with single-focused attention and rely upon quick reflexes and accuracy. The owl sees in the dark, appears as if out of thin air, and strikes with deadly precision. The pike attacks with swift efficiency. Both bring quick death to their victim, and as such, act as the reaper, the usher to the realm of the dead. What would it be like to see what must be done—and do it—with no hesitation? What would it be like to implicitly trust our instinct, intuition, and senses? What would it be like to be as sure and true in focused action as the nocturnal owl hunting, or the pike targeting its prey? What would it be like to lay aside indecisiveness, self-recrimination, and self-doubt? Owl and Pike are our teachers.

Owl is also a symbol for the manifestation of wisdom and insight. Owl has the ability to see in the dark, and take off and land silently. A revered bird in many cultures, owl is a power animal of Athena, Diana, Hecate, Lilith, and Merlin. Sophia and Owl work together as keepers of high wisdom. The idea of balance and justice also applies here and is represented by the vestal virgin (one possible representation of Virgo). She represents discrimination, ethical conduct, and impeccability.

We also honor the virgin goddesses Athena and Artemis, associated with martial arts, strategy, and negotiation. Both can teach us to fight and hunt with long-handled spears, and bows and arrows. Ceres, Demeter, and Persephone are this time of year's harvest goddesses. We give great gratitude and thanksgiving for the fruit and the seed we reap and store.

The harvest time is also one of intuition. The theme of remaining invisible or hidden until the appropriate time relates to a sense of "knowing" when the right opportunity presents itself, as when crops are ready. We do not want to harvest too early and bring inedible grain to the stores, yet grain that is too old will spoil too quickly. Creation works in a similar way: when we have nurtured our ideas and have safely enclosed them in the bed of reeds, we can let them flow. We put our trust into the universe, are guided by intuition, and watch for synchronicities or coincidences to let us know we are on the right path. We know our fairy godmothers will appear and help us get our ideas and dreams out there in the world. The right people show up at the right times, help is offered, we get the loan, we find an agent, and that "yes" we were waiting for comes our way.

Other powerful symbols applying to this month are the spiral of our DNA and the double helix shape. The yew also accompanies this time of year, symbolizing immortality and rebirth. It was important for our ancestors of the British Isles to have a symbol of hope and endurance as they entered the winter.

Guided Meditation

Many of the great queens of the Celts were powerful warriors, hunters, and negotiators. Artemis (or Diana to the Romans) and Athena are both skilled hunters who help us learn how to aim and shoot our arrows and meet the bull's eye of our intentions. Today, we will receive training in this.

Close your eyes, calm your breathing, and travel in your mind's eye to an expansive grove opening into a great field. It is a very warm and sunny September day. You see many women in training: some are working individually with the bow and arrow, some are in pairs and are sparring using martial arts techniques, while others are fencing or practicing with their knives, swords, and spears. All seem to be in deep concentration, honing their skills. It is impressive to see this number of women of different ages involved in physical training and the development of their prowess.

You are approached by a priestess who hands you a bow and a quiver of arrows. You politely refuse, indicating that you aren't an experienced archer. She smiles and instructs you on the correct posture, holding your bow, nocking your arrow, and beginning your practice. Although archery may be new to you in one dimension, you find yourself very adept, picking up the skills and nuances with ease. You are able to release your arrows repeatedly, getting closer and closer to the bull's eye. Take a moment to watch the other initiates practice their aim, concentration, and action. Practice a little more yourself ... (pause) Envision yourself nocking and aiming your arrows. Let the bowstring loose, and watch the arrow hit the bull's eye. Feel that success. Hear your comrades' cheers as you succeed.

Next, a stately priestess gathers everyone's attention and addresses you and your group. Everyone stops and listens.

> Dear initiates, you come here today to aim your weapons
> well. It is with focus, belief, and attention that you power
> your weapon so they will help you meet your goals.

Today we aim for the bull's eye, but the purpose is more than physical combat and strength: in wielding these weapons we are also directing our intent. Such action takes sincerity, devotion, commitment, and discipline. Attention and focus are the tools. Accuracy and aim are the means. Timeliness and trust play a role. It is in this way you activate your potential, of great value to yourselves and your communities. Look around and see your sisters. Know that you are here to support each other's personal goals. Trust that when desires are born from your heart, they are honored and supported by higher realms and the outer world. Never doubt there is enough love, light, inspiration, and encouragement for you. It is now time to take your final aim and strike the center of your hearts' desires. This is the last portal of the year for true completion. Soon you will begin anew, developing new plans, projects, desires, and dreams.

The other women steady themselves, focusing their minds on their targets. You too know it is now time to take your last shot for the year. Think clearly about what it is you have put much effort into and want to fulfill or complete. Raise your bow; it is the shape of the year so far. Take up an arrow from your quiver; it is your intent. Take a moment to deeply feel your intention. Then, see yourself nocking the arrow and taking careful aim at your goal, the dead center of the bull's eye. With controlled breath, you pull back that bowstring to the perfect tension; your arm and shoulder are confident and strong. At the precise and perfect moment, release the arrow and watch it fly through the air. You hit the target exactly in the middle of the bull's eye, right where you knew you would.

Feel your success and hear the applause from your sisters and unseen helpers. Know that your desire is met and the universe will respond. Give gratitude to your sisters, the priestess, and the grove. You walk away from it feeling happy and accomplished. When you feel ready, come back to this time and place. Slowly open your eyes, and ground and center yourself. As soon as you can, record your journey. What did it feel like to strike your mark true, without hesitation or doubt? What does it feel like to plan something and see it through to completion?

Reed Healing

Nothing can be accomplished without focus and attention. Use this month's portal to help you focus and send your energy towards your goals. While preparing for your goals, envision yourself surrounded by rushes in a marsh. You are supported until the time is ripe for your fairy godmother to find and nourish you and your dreams to fruition. Remember to apply conviction, determination, and a sense of purpose. When the time is right, a reed becomes an arrow and you are ready to aim and fire. Make your own "treatments" for your intentions.

In meditation, become a hollow reed so you can receive energy and information from higher sources. Pay attention and focus your breath. When you are happy, sing or play wooden instruments that require the breath. A whole body of work exists on sound's healing power. In my own healings, I have come up with chants, songs, and healing sounds spontaneously. Often, these sounds are those of whales, dolphins, or an owl. Sometimes, it is a vibratory sound that seems to break up negativity. Sometimes they are spontaneous sounds I have never heard or made before. The use of breath through our vocal chords is an amazing gift. Some of my students have strong "sound medicine" abilities. One uses Hawaiian chants that are very powerful and invigorating. Another uses the sounds of the animals and birds.

As the days grow shorter and autumn begins to show itself, contemplate your year. I am usually quite aware of the goal I have been focusing on over the course of the year, and also aware of whatever I need to cut away or let go of, as it impedes progress. I am also aware of what I still need to heal. In my journal, I write my last goal as if it has already occurred, imagining its completion and success—I really feel the joy and sense of accomplishment. I also write down what I believe impedes my progress and growth, and I ask the portal of Reed to take what I release and recycle the energy. I bring love and understanding to that which I still struggle with and want to heal. I know it is not possible to do everything I want when I want; I will keep moving towards forgiveness, because it is enough for right now. Try this for yourself and see how it serves you.

When you are going through big transitions in your life, use Reed energy to let go of one cycle and set the intention for the new cycle. For instance, I have often done rituals at this time of year as new stages in my children's lives appeared. My daughter has gone to college this year, and I have no choice but to let her go—I'm adapting to the "empty nest." I honor what has been and set my intention for a good beginning to the next phase in my life and hers. It's interesting; when I wrote an earlier section on Reed, I was letting my son go—he was leaving "the nest" at that time. My children are nine years apart, so now my daughter is at the same age my son was when I wrote that section!

As my daughter becomes an adult, I also begin a new phase of my life. My involvement in my children's lives has changed. I can have new dreams and aspirations. It's a very good thing, of course, though at times the empty house feels sad, and I know I have grief work to do. Rituals with Reed give me a blueprint of how to honor my grief and also honor my new excitement and freedom. I hope you can use Reed to help you navigate the changes you are going through as well.

STRAIF–BLACKTHORN

Shares with the Ngetal/Reed month

Description: Blackthorns have white flowers that open early, even before the leaves appear. This tree has black bark and vicious thorns. It can form dense thickets. The fruits are known as sloes and they ripen and sweeten only after the first frost.

Ogham: Straif ("strafe"), Ss, St, Z:

Negativity, negation, cleansing, perception

Class: Chieftain

Rune: Algiz

Protection. Do not collapse into emotion. New opportunities and challenges enter. Spiritual warrior, protect yourself from the trespasses of others and unwanted influences. Create healthy boundaries. Timing, right action, and proper conduct are true protection. Do not hide from or deny pain, but do not let it overcome you. Take responsibility for yourself. Renewal is promised.

Totems: The Grim Reaper; birds associated with death such as vultures and other carrion-eaters; the scapegoat figure; the warlock or black-magic practitioner; dark, "scary" figures such as the boogeyman

Astrology: Virgo (see page 149)

Blackthorn

The Straif/Blackthorn Month

Blackthorn shares the thirteenth lunation cycle with Reed. The Gaelic word *straif* is linked to the English word "strife." We are encouraged to seek out the positive in all that happens rather than dwell on the negative. Blackthorn teaches that although we may have no choice in the appearance of an unpleasant situation, we *do* have a choice to approach the situation as a cleansing one. A difficult and disruptive period often marks the beginning of a necessary, deep change. Negative points of view will not help. Letting go of resentment, stubbornness, and fear of change is required. In times of difficulty and challenge, meditate upon this tree and know that all cycles end. Recall the phrase "and this too shall pass"; there are lessons and riches to be discovered here, even in the middle of pain and suffering. The color for blackthorn is purple.

Blackthorn represents challenges: things may be difficult, but a new phase of renewal is promised. Keep to a vision that embraces new possibilities and commit to a strong resolve to move forward. The tree can offer protection. Seek spiritual sustenance and be willing to look towards a new direction of opportunity within the immediate chaos.

This tree's energies are related to things perceived as negative. All situations that we deem unfavorable fall under its rule. Death is the most common and biggest fear of many people. The misfortunes of destitution, illness, poverty, accident, theft, and loss scare us as well. No one wants to have to go through experiences that cause considerable grief.

War and the heinous crimes of rape, murder, and life-changing injury are intensely damaging and traumatic. We know about injustice, oppression, and genocide. On a smaller scale, we all have our personal demons to contend with: jealousy, spite, hatred, judgment, rage, prejudice, and the desire for revenge. Malevolent emotions live around us and in us. We wonder why we are like this and why the world we live in is so violent and brutal.

Blackthorn's message is that we are a species that learns from its difficulties and its challenges. We do not tend to change or do important, reflective work except through our suffering. Nor do we tend to demonstrate compassion without a grain of sand (a minor, external influence) that causes us to cultivate the beautiful pearl of of empathy. In our dark times, we tend to believe we're alone and often wallow in our own negativity. Most of us are stubborn, refusing to ask for help except when suffering has finally brought us to our knees. This is true for me, and I'm guessing it's true for you, too. The important thing is to remember that we open to the universe when we have no more answers to our suffering. Blackthorn promises that the universe has been waiting for the invitation and the opening all along. We are promised life at a new level after the chaos has passed, and it will.

Bad things can and do happen. Sometimes it appears that people deserve exactly what they get because they've brought it upon themselves. But we know too that bad things happen to good people for no apparent reason. Sometimes, people were just in the wrong place at the wrong time. The natural follow-up question is, "Why?" Truthfully, it really doesn't help us to ask why something bad or unfortunate has happened. Blackthorn reminds us that we all go through negative cycles and the occasional bad thing will happen. Once the bad shows up, straif offers us clues about the best way to navigate.

Totems, Guides, and Deities

The main totems of Blackthorn are birds and figures associated with death, such as vultures, birds of prey, the grim reaper, and to a lesser extent, the figure of the scapegoat and the Death and Devil cards of the tarot. The black-magic practitioner who chooses to do harm with his or her knowledge is also representative. Dark figures like the mobster, criminal, or the boogeyman all fit here. Representatives of evil and people in history who have committed horrible acts upon humanity fall here, as do images of Satan for Christians and the idea of Hell. In Egyptian cosmology, it was the god Seth and the snake Apopis that represented chaos and all evil things in the world.

The gods and goddesses that rule the fire, air, water, and earth elements have a destructive side as well, portrayed in natural disasters. The Hawaiian god Pele rules the volcano. Poseidon was blamed in ancient Greece for earthquakes, and several other cultures have deities who preside over tidal waves, twisters, floods, droughts, hurricanes, ice and snow storms, and bouts of intense heat and cold. The theme is the destructive counterpart to creation.

In the Celtic cosmology, the Crone is the harbinger of death and destruction. It is the crone aspect of the goddess that reigns over death and rebirth. Other such rulers are Hades and Holle of the underworld. The Egyptian Anubis is the god of death and embalming, and is the opener of the way. He is a grand protector and will help you navigate any sojourn into the underworld. He is there at your death to help you safely cross over into another realm, and will help you to navigate the tragedies in the spiral of your waking life.

Guided Meditation

Preparation

Write a list of:

Your biggest sufferings in life, starting from your childhood.

Your greatest fears.

That which you have not been able to forgive.

What you hate about others.

What you hate about the world.

What you hate about yourself.

Your greatest fears about death.

Close your eyes and center your breath. In your mind's eye, imagine you are inside of a tower of light, surrounded by a thicket of blackthorn trees so dense you can't see the landscape around you. You are seated upon a silken pillow and begin to slow your breath, close your eyes (again), and go within. In your mind's eye, you see a golden book upon your lap holding the list of all of your sufferings, hatreds, and fears. You turn to the page where you begin your lists and notice a warm and loving energy that seems to come from above; the energy surrounds you and your book. Take a moment to experience this infusion of support … (pause)

A dark figure approaches you and you feel a chill. An intense coldness has entered the space and the figure causes you to feel afraid. He is dressed in a dark robe and holds a staff. You cannot see his face; it is obscured by his hood. You recognize the figure before you as the grim reaper. You also see that he comes to this place of light merely to speak with you—you are fully protected. He sees your courage and he knows your heart. He has much to tell you. He knows everything you have written upon your pages, and wishes to speak with you. He has some fascinating perspectives you may not have considered. Listen to what he has to say—is it pertinent to your life? Is it eye-opening? … (long pause) When the conversation has finished, give the reaper your gratitude. He fades back into the unseen realm from which he came.

Next, a lovely old woman comes to you. She has white hair and wears a crown of silver and gold. She is draped in a purple robe. There is a lovely scent around her, and you hear peaceful and ethereal harp music coming from somewhere. The old woman extends her hand to you and says:

> I am an aspect of the crone. I am indeed your fairy godmother and constant guide. Today, I bring you a promise of success and rebirth, even through that which you have suffered. I am the new day, the new beginning, starting over from scratch, and rebuilding after desolation. With each new birth, you are encouraged to rebuild something better and more whole. I am here to encourage you to let

go of any bitterness, anger, and hatred. I ask you to tear
down the walls of isolation you have built in your pain
and disappointments. I tell you that all of this is but the
process necessary for the spirit to come to know itself.

She produces a bowl from one sleeve, and you sense it is filled
with enchanted water. Cupping some in her hands, she anoints the
top of your head. As you are anointed, you can feel that your percep-
tions about everything begin to change and you feel a great sense
of release from the places you have held these things—your body,
thoughts, beliefs, feelings, and energy field. You feel new hope and
courage, and are ready to begin anew, no matter what you are facing
or going through right now in your life. You give your gratitude to
the Crone.

Your time in the tower is nearing an end. Give your gratitude
for all that you have experienced. Thank the tower of light and the
blackthorns for their protection. Return to the room physically and
mentally, and ground and center yourself. When you feel ready, write
down your experiences, giving special attention to your discoveries
about your fears and negative associations. Also write down your experience with the Crone, your fairy godmother.

Blackthorn Healing

When you seek instant and powerful protection, imagine a thicket
of blackthorn all around you. The intense, sharp thorns and thick
foliage will keep you from harm.

Invoke Blackthorn's presence when you feel you are in a hopeless
and futile situation with no possible resolution. When you are ill, im-
poverished, and destitute, Blackthorn will remind you of other difficult times in your life when you felt similarly. You will be reminded
that you made your way through those times and you gained a better
understanding of life. You will receive reassurance.

Blackthorn is an ally when you know you have to go through challenges to reach your goals. She will sustain you through each difficulty, reminding you that your effort and discipline will pay off. In times like this, I breathe in the power of this tree and receive a strong knowing that the obstacles I am dancing with, within myself and without, are my friends and allies. The process of dealing with them with a sense of equanimity and acceptance helps me move through them with grace. I get closer and closer to my goals and am able to see the rainbow promised after the storm.

Look to opposing and adversarial forces as your allies. In journeys I have taken to meet Seth or other dark gods, I have come to understand their willingness to embrace my projections. It is their sacrifice, and it is with great love that they bear these negative feelings for us. As we are able to reclaim our projections one at a time, there will cease to be a need for a scapegoat. We won't be able to say the devil "made" us do anything. We will know we made conscious decisions and will become responsible. The trickster, the evil one, and the dark power are in a position to help us retrieve our own shadow. When I come across a real enemy—and thank goodness I haven't had that many—I look at myself and see if I can work with what I am projecting out towards them. Usually I can see that their behavior is motivated by fear and suspicion, and I can find that in myself. If I can metaphorically ask them to dinner and to hold a dialogue, soul-to-soul, I find I am far less reactive and judgmental. This kind of visualization doesn't involve actually inviting these people to dinner—I don't even have to become friends with them. I can choose to meet them with understanding. In this respect, enemies are like body symptoms: once understood and brought into the light, so to speak, they tend to disappear.

RUIS–ELDER

October 3–30
13th Lunation, October

Description: Elder is a small shrub of the honeysuckle family. They have green leaves with finely cut edges; large clusters of small white flowers; and black, purple, or red berries.

Ogham: Ruis ("roush"), R: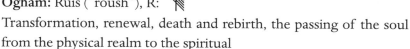
Transformation, renewal, death and rebirth, the passing of the soul from the physical realm to the spiritual

Class: Shrub

Rune: Raido ⟨R⟩
The journey, right action, movement towards healing and self-change, priorities, shamanism, the soul's journey

Totems and Guides: Cranes, storks, and the ibis; the crone aspect of the goddess

Astrology: Libra, September 22–October 23, ♎︎
    "I balance," a cardinal air sign of masculine polarity
    Symbol: the balance or scales of justice, the sun on the horizon, equal balance between night and day
    Ruling planet: Venus ♀, the 7th house of the chart
    Body Parts: Rules the kidneys and lower back

Elder

Colors: lighter blues, pink, and soft rose

Keywords: balance, equality, harmony, negotiation, love, companionship, partnership, justice

The Ruis/Elder Month

This month marks the last of the harvest and gathering of the seeds that will be saved and planted next spring. We are grateful for the food we'll store in order to survive the winter. It is a time to take stock of the year and compost whatever is leftover. It is a time to be grateful to the ancestors for their blessings and gifts, but it is also a time to release any of their weaknesses, legacies, traumas, or unhealthy beliefs stored in our DNA and memories. Elder's theme is the end in the beginning and the beginning in the end. It is a great time for personal withdrawal, retrospection, and release. Elder is related to transformation, often through death or love. Another potent plant helper here is Myrtle. Both have to do with beginnings and endings. This lunation is called the Blood Moon and its color is red.

The preceding year can be composted into energy that will fuel the new. The powers of death and rebirth are strong, and we are guided through the mystery of our own personal transformations. We can release energy into new forms and possibilities as we let go of old ideas, outworn patterns, or stagnant relationships. We surrender to the process of winter.

Elder is the threshold month and also a corridor. Take time to review your year. Celts considered elder trees "Witch trees," and it was believed that elder clan members or wise ones took up residence in an elder tree as a dryad. These wise ones are the voices of our ancestors and can give you guidance. Take the time to listen. Call on other powerful elder deities—the goddess Maat for balance and discernment, and Hecate the crone for the healthy composting of what no longer serves. This month is the time to honor our grandmothers for their years of experience and their wise blood. It is time to seek knowledge of ancient ways and to reconnect with your ancestry.

Totems, Guides, and Deities

Cranes, storks, and the ibis rule here. These wonderful birds are symbols for our soaring spirits. To the Celts, the sight of a crane foretold a new life or a death—hence the idea of the stork delivering babies. Cranes were the repository of the mystical moon wisdom of the Celts. The crane bag of the ancient druids held charms, incantations, language, stories, myths, songs, ogham script, and runic symbols. "Crane bag" was also the term used for the collective wisdom of the druidic adepts. Cranes are closely related to the feminine principle and represent higher vision and the use of the elevated intellect. The great blue heron is a majestic bird found in wetlands across North America, and was of spiritual significance to several indigenous tribes. The Celtic Crane corresponds to the great ibis-headed god, Thoth, in the Egyptian pantheon. Thoth is a master healer, scribe, and communicator of wisdom and humor. He is the holder of the highest wisdom, and honors the moon and serves lunar principles.

Many cultures hold cranes in high esteem due to their ritualistic approach to mating and territory defense. Indeed, a crane's dances of love or of aggression are striking and elegant. Cranes mate for life, and have long been symbols of parental devotion and fidelity. As a totem, Crane is both graceful and fierce. It was associated with transformation and divination or oracles, and was a companion to the Lady of the Lake. The Celts studied these birds for symbolic images out of which grew the ogham shapes. They used the shifting patterns of their legs as a source of divination. Most Celtic heroines at one time assumed the shape of the crane.

The Egyptian goddess Maat represents Libra, holding the scales of justice and balance. She stands for fairness and equality. Ancient Egyptians believed that when a person died, their soul was weighed on a divine scale against her sacred feather. The results of the measurement were recorded by her husband, Thoth, and determined whether a person was worthy enough to pass into the afterlife. She represents order within the cosmos and can help us judge and discriminate wisely. She restores harmony after chaos.

Hecate is the Greek goddess of the crossroads and works with the energy of Scorpio. Here, as the Crone, she helps us release and cut away the debris of what we have created. She guides us through the corridors of darkness, death, and rebirth. The names for the darker aspect of the crone in Ireland were the Morrigan, Badb, Macha, and Maeve. These goddesses were said to shapeshift into crows or ravens and would hover over battlefields as harbingers of death to those fighting below. In Scotland, the crone was called the Great Hag or the Cailleach Bheur. Other names were Carline, Mag-Moullach, or Beira. In Wales, she was known as Cerridwen. In Britain, she was Morgan La Fey or Morgana. Unique to Ireland was the Cailleach, or the Sheela na Gig with her blatant sexual image: a squatting hag whose hands opened her yawning vulva.

All crone figures are represented during this month. We would do well to honor those elders in our lives and listen to their stories—they have much to teach us. This is a time to look at the death of another year, and consider our own mortality. The Celts did not view death as an ending, but as a further step into one's becoming. Here, the crone also represents rebirth.

Guided Meditation

Take a moment to breathe deeply and center yourself. Close your eyes and go deep within. Set the intention to communicate with your ancestors and reconnect with your homeland and lineages.

Read the following letter to the ancestors:

> Greetings to you, my beloved ancestors. I have questions
> about my lineage I would love for you to answer to sate
> my personal curiosity, and out of a desire to connect with
> you on a deeper level.
>
> What were your names? Where were you born?
> Where did you live? What special places did you claim
> for yourself? What were your joys and sorrows, your

dreams and aspirations? How did you die? Where did you die and where are you buried? How far did you travel in a lifetime? I can look to myself and see that some of the answers live in me. What was in you has indeed been passed down to me and my children (*if you have any*)... and I am grateful.

I know the beginning of time exists in me. It is the same saline ocean in my cells and my memories. The earth, air, fire, and water live within me. The four directions live in me as does the great Mother Goddess. Above and below live in me. I feel the beat of the drum across continents, across oceans, across the color of skin and across the shape of the eye. My mouth still makes song sounds and answers the call of spirit that my tribe knew so well. All the stories ever told resound in the blood and bones of my body, in the beat of my heart space, and in the sound of my soul drum.

In the name of progress over eons of time, we forgot how to steward our home. We killed off the ceremony that kept Mother Earth alive and well. We killed off the communities that dwelt in circles; we no longer sought to commune with the wisdom in the mysteries. We left the circle and walked only in a straight line. We forgot to be thankful. We forgot to listen. We forgot to pay attention. We turned our backs on the Great Mother and laid waste to the land in our greed and shortsightedness. We forgot that we already lived in paradise.

This is true of myself, my parents, and their parents through generations. This is true of the places they came from and the cultures they embraced, endured, or suffered in. As culture after culture supplanted previous ones and attempted to end the old ways, we forgot. These are the stories of oppression, genocide, and domination.

Within these stories is the tangle of meanings that either cripple me in bigotry and falsehood, or release me to fight for a better way of being. I humbly beseech you, my ancestors, for your wisdom and your support. I will need your guidance to live well and understand the sacredness of life.

And so in my desire to claim a better way of being, I have come full circle to speak to the dead—to my ancestors. I return to the ancient tribe that sat in a circle and followed the path of the moon, prayed to the Mother Goddess, and honored their earth home as sacred. I can hear the Earth and her animals, plants, minerals, rocks, and hidden forces. I can speak with spirits and the dead. They hail me as they always have, no matter my generation or place; they have not changed. I return to the land of my ancestors and to that land's teachings. I have come home to a place that remembers; it is in my heart.

I honor my ancestors and take up the aspirations of my lineage. It is true that I live in a modern world, but it is also true that I do not have to subscribe to the lies that denigrate the earth. I may be born in a world very different than my ancestors, but I can honor their ways and remember that they held life as sacred. And I can commit to that truth.

Sit in silence for a bit after reading these words and be willing to receive images, messages, and encouragement from your loved ones, lineages, and home lands … (long pause) When you feel ready, give your gratitude, and ground and center. Afterwards, record your experiences in your journal.

Elder Healing

Write down the names of your known ancestors in your journal. Start with your maternal lineage on one page and your paternal lineage on the other. Collect stories and photographs. Dedicate an altar to those loved ones who have passed on, and be receptive to receiving messages from them in dreams, synchronicities, guided meditations, and waking revelries.

Study and read about your places of origin. Read about the original indigenous spirituality of these places. Study your original language or, better yet, travel there.

Begin inner dialogues with the people you had relationship issues with, alive and dead. Have talks that aren't about who was "right" or "wrong"; instead, speak from the soul, to the other person's soul. Actively forgive and heal these relationships. Elder will support this process.

Elder represents regeneration as it regrows damaged or cut branches easily and roots and grows rapidly from any part of itself. Whenever you begin anew, meditate with Elder and follow her example.

Take up the spirituality that best suits you. Study, listen to the music, view the art, and read the myths from that particular tradition.

Talk to your elders ... especially your grandparents or great-grandparents, if you have healthy relationships with them. Write down their stories. Ask them about their greatest lessons and most precious memories. Have them tell you about their relatives who have passed on and any family stories they can remember. Your living elders are a rich source of information. Donate your time, and visit with the elders in nursing homes. Gather their wisdom.

On the two occasions I have asked for intervention from my ancestors, I have received amazing help. Once I asked for help for my son, who was having difficulty finding a job. The very next day at nine AM, two calls came in, both offering him a job. The other time, I asked for help so my daughter could attend the school that would best fit her needs. The first month of her high school experience was miserable, and she wanted to transfer. She was an excellent student, and it was not like her to come home in tears every day. She wanted to be in a school that offered the best program in the arts, but she was on the waiting list. On the last day that the school district would allow changes, I called. I was told she was ninth on the list and the secretary told me she probably wouldn't get in. After hanging up, I immediately asked my ancestors for their intervention, addressing each one I could think of. The very next hour, the school called me and said she had been accepted! In my times of need, my ancestors definitely respond! Although I thought it was very weird, I feel extremely grateful for my ancestors' help.

Cedar Grove

ᏟᎻᎬ ᎠᎯᏘ

October 31
Samhain, Hallowmas,
All Hallow's Eve, Halloween

Ogham: Koad (ea, ch), the Shears ✕
The Grove, the Temple, silence, initiation, reconnection with spirit, communicating with and appreciating the dead, recommitment to your spiritual path

Rune: the blank rune ⬚
Unlimited potential, wide-open possibilities, the blank canvas, the sum of all totalities

Holiday: Samhain, Hallowmas, Halloween, October 31

The Day, October 31

Halloween is one of the most important times of the year in the Celtic tree calendar. There is no particular tree that stands for this day; rather, a grove of sacred trees is its representation. Whether it be a grove of cedars, oaks, or fir, ancient Celts gathered and would invoke magic. The circle would be especially powerful because it was held by the force of many trees, creating a sacred and honored space. In creating this space now, we may enter between worlds—the veil is very thin at this time of year. Names for this day are Samhain, Samhuinn, Halloween, Hallowmass, All Hallow's Eve, and Calan Gaeaf.

All these days commemorate the dead, and death and rebirth are the themes of this special day.

Samhain marks the end and beginning of the Celtic year. The period from October 31 to November 2 was a time when regular structure and order were put aside and chaos and mayhem were encouraged. Time was abolished for the three days of this festival, and people did crazy things. Men dressed as women and women as men. Farmers' gates were unhinged and left in ditches, people's horses were moved to different fields, and children would knock on neighbors' doors for food and treats. This tradition is still carried out in our custom of trick-or-treating on Halloween.

Behind the madness of this day lay a deeper meaning, however. The druids knew the veil between this world and the one of the ancestors was temporarily drawn aside. If one was prepared, this was a time for making contact with spirits of the departed, seen as sources of guidance and inspiration rather than as sources of fear and dread. The dark moon—the time when no moon can be seen in the sky—was the moon phase ruled by the crone aspect of the goddess. The crone encouraged inner vision and travel into other worlds.

Make sacred space. Light candles in the dark. Call in the spirit world. Be in silence. Honor dark places: of caves, crevices, and undercrofts deep in the earth's womb. Remember ancestors, elders, family, friends, and animals who have crossed over. Be grateful for their legacies and teachings. Some are your "backwards teachers" and have given you powerful lessons in what you don't want to be like, so you can choose a better path. Others are wonderful models for the kind of person you would like to become. All help form your becoming.

Become aware of your own personal totems, guides, and deities. These are your allies. Be sure to give them the attention and appreciation they so deserve. Make this one day a commitment of gratitude for all the help and guidance you have received from the spirit world.

The Day is tied to the blank rune of Odin, and the ogham is the Koad, signifying the grove. The grove in turn signifies akasha, referring to all knowledge—past, present and future. Here we honor the oracle and the power of divination. Scrying is an ancient Celtic art of looking into the future. Look into a bowl of water or a crystal ball and call in akashic power to enlighten you. Allow your imagination to form symbols, pictures, or impressions. These are communications from the realm of akasha.

Initiation is the theme of the Day. The process of transformation is significant. In every initiation process, there is a mystic death and rebirth. In shamanic cultures, there is a dismemberment process and a new configuration. We honor the process of reinventing ourselves to higher and wider, more expansive versions. In the alchemical cauldron, we can become enlightened spirits in service of the uplifting of consciousness. In shamanic terms, we gladly open ourselves to this process. Our personality identifies with the essential self and leaves the identity with the temporal or smaller self behind. We identify as spirit rather than body. At this juncture, the spirits are able to work through us and we can serve our communities in a greater sense. A symbolic dismemberment may occur, through an initiatory experience which marks the death of one way of being in the world, replaced with another.

In ancient Egypt, initiates went through a symbolic death during which they were buried alive for a period of hours or days. If they survived, they were considered resurrected. Today, we don't need to perform as drastic rituals as these; we may instead embrace the initiatory experience that goes along with simply being alive on the planet at this moment in time. Changes occurring right now in the Earth's electrical and magnetic fields are said to be the same energetics the ancient Egyptian pyramids and temples created for the purpose of accelerating consciousness. The intensity with which we are experiencing life is very real and purposeful. Most of us can testify to increased intensity in our lives and the sense of time flying by.

This intensity and degree of experience is causing our confusion and dissociation from all parts of the self but we can choose the alchemical process of reintegration. We are gifted with many tools in this process. We have the power of our thoughts, beliefs, words, and actions as we create our lives. Taking responsibility for these is our act of power. Dreams, symbols, poems, art, music, the use of our crystal bowls, drums and other instruments, songs, stories, the protection and guidance of our totems and spirit helpers, and our acknowledgement that we are co-creators with spirit are our helpers.

This is a day of self-initiation. Take a moment to recommit to your spiritual path. Begin again to reconnect to spirit. Take some quiet time to open to all that is, the oneness. Use prayer in whatever way is comfortable for you. Call spirit in whatever name you use. But do so, for this is the day to start anew. Be willing to enter the silence.

Totems, Guides, and Deities

This is a time to give gratitude and make time to connect to your own personal totems, guides, and deities. My special helpers have been Dolphin, Dragon, the trees, and faeries. On this day, we honor especially the crone aspect of the goddess. She has many names, but I am most familiar with Hecate and Cerridwen.

Samhain is a day to remember those dear to you who have crossed over, including your pets. Make an altar and put pictures, letters, or reminders of these special people and animals in your life. Take a bit of time to sit in silence before your altar and listen for any messages.

This is also a time when it is helpful to send healing energy to those who are ill, infirmed, or suffering. In meditation, imagine white light surrounding them, and see them returning to good health.

Think of your ancestors and your places of origin. Remember the indigenous teachings from these places. Give gratitude to the spiritual traditions from around the world that have meaning for you. Think of sacred places. You can imagine yourself at these sites receiving particular messages and energies, if you like. Ask your ancestors for help when you need it and always give them your gratitude.

Travel in meditation to places in nature that have special meaning to you. You could return to a special tree from your childhood, find a grove of trees to sit in, or sit inside your home and meditate on the healing power of trees. Whatever you choose to do, give your gratitude and love.

Buy things made by indigenous people around the globe. Doing so helps support their way of life and their spiritual practices. I believe that those who pray to and honor the unseen realms help to keep our world in order. Learn how to make something with your hands. If you carve a pipe or weave a basket, it will slow you down and the wood or plant fiber will communicate with you. If you study a particular culture, try to learn how to make something with your own hands from this culture.

Guided Meditation

Take this Samhain journey to the Isle of Healing. Imagine yourself standing before a sea marking the boundary between the seen and the unseen realms. It is from this place that you will journey. It is from this place that you will call your beloved dead. You will also travel from this place between worlds and meet your dearly departed friends, family, and ancestors.

Close your eyes and still yourself. Feel yourself relax as you breathe more slowly and deeply. Let the cares of your day melt away as you find yourself becoming quiet and receptive.

You find yourself on a boat traveling in dark water. Speak aloud the names of your departed ones silently to yourself ... (pause) With each name spoken, you come closer and closer to the isle of your reunion. Loved ones you have lost are setting sail at the same time from their own dimension. You all plan to arrive on this special land between the worlds. As you travel, you sense your loved ones moving closer and closer to you.

As the veil parts in the mist, you also invite ancestors whose names you do not know to join you. You become aware they have much to share with you. Further ahead, you see a green island. Repeat the names of your loved ones as you get closer and closer.

The boat arrives at the island and you step on the shore. Take a moment to feel your feet on the land and center yourself. Open all your senses to this special place. Feel the earth, inhale the air, and follow the path up to a grove of trees you see standing on a small hill. The dead are arriving too, and they are very happy that you have not forgotten them. They have missed you terribly.

As you enter the magical grove, you take notice of who is here. You recognize your loved ones and your ancestors. Who are they? Who has you called to this place? (long pause)

Perhaps there is a special conversation you need to have to be at peace. Perhaps you need something from someone here. Perhaps someone needs something from you. Follow your heart and find the loved ones you need to speak to. Have faith that your loved ones will let you know if they need to speak to you. Here, ideas and feelings may be freely exchanged, and you don't have to keep your guard up or hold on to past grievances.

What do they have to say? Here you can make magic that can change things for all of you. Take your time. Decide between yourselves what that change could be ... (long pause)

This place is very special; you can focus on the changes in your life you would like to see or make happen. What do you want to see happen in the coming year? In this place between worlds, the magic is so strong that you can feel these changes already beginning to manifest ... (pause) Look into the future and see those changes as though they have already occurred ... (pause) Feel the change; experience it, take it in ...

You hear music and sense that a great dance is beginning. Spirits swirl around you and you feel caught up in the movement, twirling from partner to partner. Some souls you recognize and some you don't. Throughout the dance, you hear the dead remind you to savor your sweet life. They remind you that life on Earth is quite short. All the while, you dance and sway to a most magical drumbeat, and hear a most mystical tune.

Go deep inside and listen to the loving messages from your departed loved ones. Feel their deep love, gratitude, and support. It feels joyful to see them and talk with them again, and you know in your heart that they are not lost to you.

As the music comes to an end, you form a large circle, all holding hands. Give your loved ones and ancestors your love and gratitude. Nod to each being in the circle. All the souls nod back at you and let you know they will never be far from you. They send you a message of love. Their hopes and dreams live in you.

It is time to say your goodbyes and return to the boat that will sail you across the dark seas. You feel renewed and encouraged as you disembark.

It is now time to return from this sacred journey and return to this time and space. Ground and center, and when you are ready, open your eyes. Record your journey in your journal.

Healings for the Day

Forgiveness is the strongest medicine. Meeting all loss and grief with understanding is powerful and can be life-changing. Dreams can also be tremendously helpful in healing. As an example, I would like to share a powerfully moving dream that I received and have since used as a blueprint for working with and healing the shadow side of the self:

I was standing upon a cement barricade in the ocean. Three huge, frightening monsters rose out of the water and moved up to a park area near the shoreline. The people there panicked and were running, hysterically yelling and blaming me for invoking these beings from the ocean. The monsters were so immense and terrifying that there was no way I could run fast enough to get away from them. As they stood above me, looking like they could reach down, grab me, and devour me without a second thought, the only thing I could think of was to invite them to dinner.

Suddenly, there was a lovely dinner laid out on a long dining table filled with food and nicely set for four. To my amazement, the three huge monsters seemed to like the idea! They sat down in a polite manner and ate with me. We had an enjoyable dinner, and by the time we were finished, they had shrunk in size and remained very civilized. They thanked me and made their way back to the sea.

Upon waking from that dream, I realized it was a map for how to bring to "the table" that which is frightening, overbearing, or troubling. When these kinds of energies are invited out of the dark depths of your unconscious, treated with kindness, fed, attended and listened to, and met with understanding, they have no need to puff themselves up, frighten us, or otherwise derail our lives. When I have troubling feelings, thoughts, or behaviors, I "invite them to dinner."

Like many people, my biggest fear is death. I often invite Death in her many guises to the table. She may appear as a scary hag, in her male form as one of the four horses of the apocalypse, or as the grim reaper. Over dinner, however, she becomes an ally and is often the wisest of all. She reminds me to live the life I have been given to its fullest. She explains that we can either view life through the lens of our fears, failures, and losses (limiting our perception and adding to our misery), or we can choose to make friends with negativity. We can ask our bogeymen to dinner, feed them in a good way with love and understanding, and see our life as an adventure—it's a choice. Representatives of the negative or dark side (or death itself) can become our allies; they have much to offer us. Every year at Samhain, I am reminded to invite my biggest fears, perceived enemies, and challenges to dinner. In Mexico, dinner is brought to the gravesites on *El Día de los Muertos*, the synthesis of Spanish and indigenous Mexican traditions. In certain Native American traditions, a spirit plate is always served, placed at the table for the ancestors.

It is possible to commune with the dead, and it often comes through dreams, synchronicities, and guided visions or journeys. Once, in a guided journey, my sister-in-law met with her deceased father, who appeared as her guardian angel. After having the dream, she felt a wonderful sense of relief, protection, and reunion. Another time, right before her mother's death, we decided to visit with her mother's spirit. Her mother was in her late nineties and was very ill, hanging on by a thread. She was deaf, almost completely blind, and unable to communicate.

Late one November, my sister-in-law and I entered a guided meditation together with the intention of speaking to her mother's soul and giving her permission to die if it was what she needed in order to let go. My sister-in-law told her mother that if she was ready, she could go. Her mother's concern seemed to be that she might still need her. This information struck my sister-in-law as humorous— really, she had been taking care of her for years as her health deteriorated. She assured her mom that she would be all right and that it was her time to go. We asked her sister, who had died of cancer, to stay close to her mom and help her in her transition. As we came out of the journey I asked her when she would be ready to let her mom go. She said, "After Christmas." Then she said, "No, actually I can let her go before Christmas if that's her wish." Her mother passed on in the next few weeks, before Christmas.

The communication with my sister-in-law and her mother was full of love, gratitude, and sweetness. Speaking soul to soul can be exactly like this. And the soul doesn't have to be deceased; both souls can be alive, and you can speak to souls that are dead, as well as souls hovering in between.

The Day is a perfect time to have conversations with people in the kindest and most civilized way. It wasn't necessary for my sister-in-law's mom to hang on any longer, but she needed her daughter's permission and gentle release.

Another friend of mine chose to have many inner conversations, soul to soul, with her angry and contentious husband when they were going through a divorce. She kept saying that she knew at the soul level that he was a good man, and that he would do the right thing by her. She was quite amazed when in fact he *did* act in a fair and equitable manner, rather than fight hard to come out on top, as was his usual routine. If there are people in your life whom you have issues with, try talking at a soul level with them. Seek their forgiveness and give them yours. This inner work often has wonderful and powerful results, and you won't have to confront anyone directly, possibly causing more conflict. Sometimes it is impossible to have an in-person conversation with someone who won't or can't forgive.

As mentioned before, I have asked for help from the ancestors at times. I've said their names and asked for intercession. In return, they have answered and helped me. I encourage you to open up a line of communication—you will be greatly blessed and enriched. It is good not to feel alone. The ancestors, our deceased loved ones, and even the souls of those we share life with at the core all want the same thing. We feel better when we forgive each other and create loving and helpful relationships.

The portal of this day opens up the possibilities for conversations and communications that are healing and uplifting. We miss our loved ones, and it is possible to connect with them in such a way that we know death is not the end and is not final.

APPENDICES

APPENDIX A

The Vowels and the Consonant and Vowel Combinations

Ailim: Silver Fir/Pine

POST WINTER SOLSTICE

Description: Native to Europe, this tall, slender tree is a member of the pine family and has dense foliage with silver needles. The needles are usually soft, blunt, and fragrant, and are evenly distributed around every branch (firs are soft, spruces are not). Cylindrical cones grow upright on the branches. These trees grow in the mountains on upper slopes that overlook the surrounding forests.

Ogham: Ailim ("al'yem," "AHL-m"), A: ╾┼╾

Foresight, higher perspective

This is one of the tallest of the British trees, and because it grows to great heights and can see over great distances, it encourages us to reach above or to rise above things in order to reach a higher understanding. Fir encourages us to take the high road and look at the big picture. This tree promises clear-sightedness. We are encouraged to learn from past mistakes and to take care in new choices. Clear-sighted progress is indicated. We are helped to put things into perspective. We see things from above and are given a spiritual infusion of understanding.

Its color is silver. This tree links you to your silver thread, which symbolizes your awareness of your own spiritual journey. This cord allows you to fly during astral travel and return to your body. This illuminates your connection to your Higher Self and higher dimensions of love and light. It represents the ability to see into other realms and it encourages inner vision. We gain insight and expanded awareness. We receive messages in our dreams and visions. The tree also indicates change for the better and peak experiences.

Class: Shrub

Rune: Ansuz [ᚨ]

Signals, messages, and gifts

Ansuz is called the messenger rune, and stands for connection with the divine or a higher order. It is also connected to the god Loki, the ancient trickster from the Norse pantheon. He is the *heyoka* of the Lakota. Expect the unexpected! Whatever the message is, it is a call to something new. Let go of what is not working. It is time to begin inner work. Listen to messages from synchronicities. Make time to commune with spirit. Follow your intuition.

Holidays: Winter Solstice

Totems: The fir is an evergreen and symbolizes the Great Mother in her three aspects of maiden, mother, and crone, as it appears to never die. In Ireland, names for the goddess are Domnu, Danu, Anu, Ana, Banba, Eriu, Artha, Brigit, Grainme, Macha, Morrigu, and Sheela na Gig. In Wales, she was Blodeuwedd, Arianrhod, Mona, Rhiannon, Gwenhwyfer and Cerridwen. In Scotland, she was the Cailleach, Bera, Brigit, Cale, Carline, Scota, and Mag Moullach. In England, she was the White Lady, Ana, Dana, Amma, Annis, Artha, Albe, Graine, Ker, Madron, Modron, Mab, Morgana, Rigantona, Epona, Guinevere, Vivienne, the Lady of the Lake, Elaine, and Nimue (Jones, 7).

Healing

This tree can be used to attract prosperity. It has been called the birth tree and can be used for protection for mothers and babies during childbirth. Set your intention that all goes well, and burn a few needles prior to the birth.

Trees can offer help energetically and you can apply energetic medicine from this tree for many of your needs. Use Fir's energetic medicine to treat cuts, burns, colds and coughs, and as a laxative. Simply hold out your hand, invite in Fir's etheric energy, and apply it just above the place that needs it, about three inches from the body.

Ask for Fir's assistance when using divination to seek clarity in your life. As this tree can see the bigger picture, it may know something you don't. This tree is a wonderful source of divine assistance. You may be able to see the past, the present, and the future.

When faced with a challenging situation or person, I ask Fir to expand my vision and take me to a higher vantage point. I imagine myself on the very top of the tallest fir or pine tree, on the tallest hill. Sometimes an eagle comes and sits upon my shoulder. I then can see into a situation or the other person's point of view with new eyes, becoming aware of things I wasn't before. The new information can change my perception and I become far less reactive, seeing into what may be helpful.

When very lonely or separated from loved ones, call the energy of this tree and invoke the Great Goddess. She will come and provide you with the mothering and love you are missing. Imagine her love as a soothing pink blanket of energy that she spreads over you. Allow her loving field to absorb your loneliness; replace that energy with hope and light. It may become clear to you that from this insecure and depressed position, you cannot very well evaluate your life. Wait until your mood is better and look again. In the meantime, be patient with your low mood, knowing it will pass. Be kind to yourself.

Ohn: Gorse/Furze

SPRING EQUINOX

Description: Though this shrub is a needle-bearing evergreen, it does not produce cones. It has bright yellow flowers that bloom in March, and is associated with the sun. It has very dense and prickly branches and sharp, spiny leaves.

Ogham : Onn or Ohn ("on," "UHN"), O: ╪

Collecting, sweetness, hope, persistence

This shrub often stands alone so it can claim as much sunlight as possible. There is no month within the year that it doesn't retain its bloom, and it is persistent in its growth. It symbolizes abundance and generosity. Be generous. In gratitude, share your abundance with others. Gorse links the inner and the outer worlds with fulfillment and abundance. It also represents the sweetness of honey as its flowers are rich with pollen and nectar for the bees. Gorse represents the gathering together of what is required to move towards a goal or destination. The key word here is "collecting." Gorse is also related to the magpie with its eye for shiny, golden treasure. It is also a valuable guide on one's spiritual journey. Its color is yellow-gold.

Class: Chieftain

Rune: Othila ⏃

Separation, retreat, inheritance (acquisition and benefits, real property)

A peeling-away is called for. Letting go or severing from that which no longer serves. A benefit received may be derived from something you must give up. The separation will free you to become a truer version of yourself. It might be necessary for you to retreat. It supports you to know when and how to make a change. It helps you with the firmness you may need to carry out your plan.

Holiday: The day before the equinox is often called the Day of Gorse. Spring Equinox and Lammas (Lughnasadh).

Totems: Gráinne, Arianrhod, the maiden aspect of the goddess, Bel, Lugh, the fairies, bees and honey.

Healing

Use Gorse to sweep away evil influences. Make a broom of its branches and sweep away what you no longer need. You may also use it to sweep away winter as a way of welcoming spring.

In old times, gorse was used to remedy depression. Use it energetically to work with hopelessness and despair. The golden flowers bring in the sunlight and offer renewed hope.

In the same way that it draws bees to its scent, color, and nectar, you can use Gorse to attract a combination of forces and possibilities. The yellow flowers attract life energy and can assist you in your growth and support you as you move towards fulfilling your potential. When focusing on what you want to manifest, use Gorse to attract your intended goals.

Use Gorse energy when you come together with others, to encourage cooperation and working together towards a goal. Just having sprigs of gorse around can remind you of this sweet intention.

The spring equinox heralds the return of spring and the light. Persephone returns to her mother, Demeter, from the underworld. The sap rises in trees and plants. The young stag begins to grow its antlers. Young men and women become ripe for their first sexual experiences. Life is filled with new promise. Give your gratitude for the rebirth of the life cycle. You will be surprised at how healing the act of giving gratitude can be. Many people keep a gratitude journal and write something they are grateful for every day.

Ur: Heather/Mistletoe

SUMMER SOLSTICE

Description: Heather is an evergreen shrub that grows close to the ground in dense clusters. It is found on the moors (floodplains) of Great Britain. Heather has grayish, low, hairy stalks, broomlike branches, and needlelike leaves. Its tiny blossoms are shaped like bells and grow in long clusters called spikes. The flowers are purple, white, or orange.

Mistletoe is a parasite plant that grows on other trees. It is an evergreen with thickly clustered leaves and tiny yellow flowers that bloom in February and March. It has shiny white berries, plentiful at Yule. Mistletoe was used as a sacred ceremonial plant, especially when found growing on an oak tree.

Ogham: Ur ,Ura ("oor," "oorah"), U: ≢

Healing and spiritual development
Heather represents the gateway linking the earth and the spirit world. Mistletoe is known as a panacea and represents the invisible life essence when shared with its host, the Oak. Together, Heather and Mistletoe represent closer contact with the spirit world, resulting in healing. Express gratitude. Open up to love, dreams, passion, and generosity. Honor the faerie world. Healing comes through contact with the divine. This ogham's color is purple.

Class: Peasant/Chieftain

Rune: Uraz ᚢ

Strength
This is the rune of passage. You have outgrown the life you're currently living. Growth may involve a descent into darkness as part of the cycle of renewal. Death and rebirth; release may be called for. A firm sense of principle and humility will give you strength. Your soul and the universe support new growth. Endings and new beginnings.

Adapt yourself to the demands of the time. Through loss comes opportunity. Include service in your life.

Holiday: Summer Solstice

Totems: Isis, Arianrhod, Venus, the mother or pregnant aspect of the mother goddess, Mabon, Pan, or the Green Man

Healing

Gather Heather to manifest wishes. Place Heather under your pillow to stimulate dreams. This plant is useful when contacting spirits. Gather heather and mistletoe for healings. Its branches were used for green and yellow dye. In the past, heather was used to dissolve gall and kidney stones, deal with internal disorders, and soothe insect stings. You can use this plant energetically to work with any of these problems. Heather twigs were used for brooms, both in energetic and actual cleaning. Make a charm of heather, as it is both protective and brings good luck.

When mistletoe was found on an oak, it was said to carry the life essence of the gods. Use it in the celebration of the male potency, as represented by such figures as the Green Man. It also represented survival and immortality, as it usually lives beyond the lifespan of its host, and also grows up and above its host. The white berries represent the seed of the Green Man and the red berries of the holly represent the Goddess and her menstrual cycles. Together they represented the continuity of life and immortality. Include both in your rituals when trying to conceive.

When you seek balance for your male/female attributes, bring in the energy of Mistletoe. Give mistletoe as a gift to bring good fortune. Use it for rituals of change and transformation. Medicinally, it was used as a sedative, a fertility aid, an antidote for poison, and a treatment for epilepsy.

Eadha: White Poplar/Aspen
AUTUMN EQUINOX

Description: The leaves of these trees seem to tremble or quiver in the wind. They have long, clustered catkins that release thousands of cottonlike seeds. Leaves are small and oval- or heart-shaped, and turn yellow in autumn. These trees grow very quickly and have huge root systems that need plenty of space to grow.

Ogham: Eadha, Eadhadh, Edad ("ayda," "EH-yuh"), E: ≣
Adversity
How do we face adversity? Consider these trees: they are hardy, fast growing, and strongly resistant. Be courageous and you can overcome and endure your troubles. When life gives us problems, doubts, and fears, we need endurance and courage. Success after troubles is promised. Aspen is the one most concerned with material realities. It provides spiritual strength to help us face unexpected or harsh situations. This tree provides shielding against difficulty and can protect you from death, injury, and misfortune. It has a close connection with the winds. The tree's limbs and leaves make noise when blown in the wind, and they are thought to carry messages from the spiritual realm. These messages are in a special language you can hear. Its color is silver white.

Class: Shrub

Rune: Ehwaz [M]
Movement, progress
This rune has to do with transit, transition, physical shifts, and movement towards new dwelling places, new attitudes, and a new life. It encourages steady development over time. The keyword is "improvement," which could apply to a business or an idea. You have progressed far enough to feel a sense of safety. Share your good fortune with others.

Holiday: Autumn Equinox

Totems: the horse pulling the sun across the sky; the sun fosters new life and illuminates all things in its light; Herne the hunter and his relationship to animals and his responsibility as a steward of the land; the Stag God, Cernunnos, that gives up his life; the Green Man and his impending sacrifice; the Crone aspect of the Goddess

Healing

Aspen and white poplar were used to alleviate fevers. The buds, bark, and leaves contained salicylates, similar to aspirin. They wereused for earaches, asthma, and coughs. You can call in the energetic properties of these trees to effect healing.

These trees will get you through difficult times. After an ecological disaster they are one of the first to grow (besides alder), so they have a strong, stabilizing effect and can start a healing process. Bring the energy of Poplar and Aspen into your meditations after a shocking event or situation, so you can begin stabilizing yourself and initiate the healing process.

Aspen and Poplar offer you a strong sense of perseverance and courage. While it may take hard work and tenacity to defend yourself from an opposing force, these trees will supply you with the inner strength and resolve that you need to meet a struggle. Success and victory are quite possible.

When you are worried about theft, call in the energy of Aspen for protection; it also offers protection when traveling. Poplar will also protect you as you travel and communicate with other realms.

When you are near an aspen or a poplar, take a moment to listen to the sounds it makes. Listen to its whispers—it has messages for you. If nothing else, simply listening will calm and center you.

Ioho: Yew

RETURN TO THE WINTER SOLSTICE

Description: This tree grows in such a way that it allows itself to stay in the same place for centuries. Its branches grow down into the ground to form new stems, and these form the trunks of new trees. Thus, when the central trunk of the original tree becomes old and decays, a new tree will grow from the old one and continue to feed from the same roots. This tree has a similar appearance to a fir tree. It is an evergreen with flat needles; the female tree has bright red berries. It rarely grows in a forest with other trees.

Ogham: Ioho, Iodho, Idad, Iodhadh, Ido ("yoho," "EE-yoh"), I, J, Y: ䷀
Rebirth, death, transition, endings, reincarnation
You will often find a yew tree in the cemeteries in Britain. They are far older than the cemeteries themselves, and some are known to be more than 2,000 years old. Yew is linked with the island of Iona off the coast of Scotland, whose traditions include the ideas of rebirth and reincarnation. No matter what is encountered in life, a new start always presents itself again. Embrace change. In every ending is a new beginning. Complete change in life, direction, or attitude. Ever- lasing life and reincarnation. This tree and its parts are poisonous. It connects us to the dead and our ancestry. Related to Samhain, death, divinity, immortality, longevity, and change. This tree reminds us that space and time are inventions, but not necessarily the true foundation of reality. Its color is dark green.

Class: Chieftain

Rune: Isa ⏐
Standstill, withdrawal, ice
Do not stubbornly persist through willpower. Now is not the time to forge ahead. Practice patience. You may find yourself in a period of forced inaction. Use your courage and wisdom to surrender. Go within to seek renewal at the deepest level. Seek solitude. Wait for the thaw. Spring always returns after winter.

Holiday: Winter Solstice Eve, Yule

Totems: The Crone aspect of the Goddess, Taliesin, Badb, Banba, Cailleach Beira, Hecate, Hel/Holle, Pluto, the Grim Reaper, Dagda, Hermes, Lugh, or Odin. It is known as one of the five great trees of Ireland—the Tree of Ross. I find special meaning in this, as my father's name was Ross, my son and my nephew have the middle name of Ross, and my other nephew's son is named Ross.

Healing

Yew trees grow mainly in the Pacific Northwest and northeastern parts of the United States. When I can't visit an actual tree, I turn to books and the Internet to see pictures of it. Then, with my eyes closed, I travel to the tree in my mind's eye. I have ancestors buried in the British Isles and sometimes I travel to their burial places through the roots of my internal Yew tree. I ask them questions or simply listen to the things they want to communicate. Usually they give me a sense of renewal, hope, and encouragement. Sometimes they have regrets, but they always communicate how life is so precious and how they wish they had understood that better when they were alive.

Yew can encourage and help you develop your psychic ability. Learn to listen to your own inner voice. Once, when looking for a teaching job, I was told there were no jobs available. I sat in the employment office at the public schools building for a moment just to gather my thoughts. Then, in a quiet voice, I heard the words, "Sit down and wait." I thought it was crazy—I had just been told that finding a job here wasn't going to happen. Again I heard the words, "Sit down and wait." So I did. It felt odd to be sitting there just trusting the voice. I couldn't imagine what was going to happen. In about fifteen minutes, a little man came out and asked if he could help me. I told him I wanted a teaching job. He told me to come into his office, and he would help me. He was hiring, and he eventually offered me a job! I was to start the next week. How's that for proof that listening to the inner voices can help? Of course, I'm not talking about voices or impulses people have that sometimes encourage them to do bad things. Clearly, this voice was helping me. That helpful origin is one way I can distinguish whether to listen.

Bring this tree into your sacred space when you use your divination tools. When you require a dream of special significance and power, invoke the yew and ask for its help.

These trees understand longevity. If you seek counsel on how you can live long and in good health, spend time with Yew. Ask this tree to provide physical and emotional strength during trying times. Give your gratitude and give something to the tree directly, if possible. Within your mind's eye, you may water it, feed nutrients to its roots, or give it healing energy through your hands. This tree also understands how to best move through change, and it represents our immortal spiritual aspect. Yew teaches us that forms change, but the circle of life remains.

The yew tree was planted in graveyards next to the graves of wise leaders. It was said to hold their knowledge and wisdom, making it available for the future benefit of the community. The energy of this tree can provide you with solutions and ideas you might never have imagined. Yew undertstands that we need help solving the problems we have created. A tree that knows how to live so long on earth, and has witnessed so much change, is a wise source of information. If you are willing to quiet yourself enough and engage this tree, an exchange of information is promised; it could be beneficial to your community or even society at large. Consider where the innovative ideas that support the sacredness of life come from—look to Yew.

The Koad: The Grove
OCTOBER 31

Description: Instead of being a single tree, the representation here is an entire grove of trees of any kind, though the oak grove has special druidic importance.

Ogham: Koad, "ea" vowel combination and "ch" or "kh" consonant combinations, ✕

All knowledge, the silence, initiation

Two crossed fingers show the shears, the ogham that represents a grove of trees, a temple, or a holy place. Druid meetings were held in the open within a circle of trees, usually oaks. These special groves of ancient times usually existed near a spring. They were sacred areas used for meetings, ceremony, ritual, and the dispensing of law and judgment. The grove holds the information of all the hidden knowledge the trees of our ancestors contain.

We seek wisdom by choosing to see past illusions. The Grove offers us insight into the nature of reality, the true principles of the universe, and unity consciousness. The Grove also gives support when we are working towards a goal for the common good. As sacred ground and the central place of balance and infinite possibility, the Grove is the void from which all things are manifested and to which all things return. Within it is the mystery. We can learn to interact with the mystery but can never explain it. The color is many shades of green.

Class: None

Rune: Odin's Rune, the Blank Rune ☐

The unknowable

This is the all-powerful and unnameable expression of oneness. It is the end and the beginning. You connect to your own true destiny. You are encouraged to have faith. You enter the silence and connect to your own soul. Evolution comes through the work of self-change. Change your thoughts, change your life. Make room for the light.

You are forever in the act of becoming. You are never-ending. Communication is possible with the divine, oneness, source, God, Goddess, spirit, first-cause, and all potentials.

Holiday: Samhain. Contact with the spirit world, ancestors, and relatives and animals who have passed on. Let go of outworn ideas, values, and plans.

Totems: Here you make connection and give your gratitude to all of your totems, guides, and deities. Invoke the power of the higher-order guides to connect you to divinity and your essential essence. These may be angels, light beings, beings of the star nations, and the many deities.

Keening was a gift from the goddess Brigit and is a highly charged form of releasing grief. Also known as *caoine*, it is a powerful mourning wail. Sound used this way is a wonderful release. Brigit was also called the fairy ghost or banshee (*bansidhe*). She is responsible for the keening said to be heard throughout the land on the night before a death. She is also said to be a protective spirit of the clan, and an ancestral deity.

All the crone aspects of the goddess belong to the grove. The crone's talismans were the moon sickles (shears) that cut the corn and the thread of life, and the cauldron of death and regeneration. She resided in the long burrows and was pregnant with the souls of the dead. Her totem was the great white sow or pig. Another representative was the frog goddess of death and regeneration. She resided in cave and rock formations and dolmens that marked the entrance to underground burrows.

Healing

Wakes, funerals, and memorials are all opportunities to celebrate the life of the deceased and to mourn. If these ceremonies can be held within a grove, all the better. The crone goddesses work with Yew energy to support you in any grief work you may encounter.

The koad represents the inner silence. Take time to meditate and connect with the divine. Ask your most powerful helpers to act as a bridge to connect you to your source: Gaia, Mother Earth, Mother Moon, and the archangels. If you do not make the time here, how will you ever hear what your inner guidance says? How will you ever reap your own ecstasy? How will you ever receive the blessing of the universal life force that replenishes and restores?

Travel in your imagination to special places of power on Earth. Some of you may have special synagogues, churches, or temples. For me, there are the many temples in Egypt in which I am able to connect with oneness and supreme spirit. I also am drawn to the stone circles of the British Isles. I have favorite groves and circles of trees which I visit in my neighborhood and in my city. Your most spiritual place may be in the deep forest or your own backyard. Take some time to connect to the energy of these places of solace. Align yourself to spirit.

Celtic tradition teaches that death is but another door. Gather around you some books about death and dying, and also read books by authors who communicate with the dead. Begin to face your fears of death with the Grove's help. The Grove will hold spiritual space for you when you contemplate the idea that your body is merely a temporary abode for spirit, and it will go on to have many more experiences in consciousness.

The Grove represents the sum total of all tree teachings. It helps you look beyond the surface and see the underlying principles of life, the spiritual and natural, the revolving patterns of the world, the seasons, and the cosmos. The Grove indicates this knowledge is already within us and that we each have our own inner grove. Take a moment to visualize this grove within yourself. Then, visualize yourself sitting at the center of your grove—this is your sacred ground. Sitting here in silence and receptivity will always provide you with the bigger picture and align you to your purpose. This alignment is especially important when you become lost in details and can't see the forest for the trees. It is from this inner place that you can create beauty, harmony, and peace. Keep coming back to this inner grove.

Once when I was betrayed by a lover, I went to a grove of trees and sat in the center. I cried and shared my shock and sense of violation. These feelings went directly into the earth and into the deep roots of the large grove. They shared the grounding of this energy from my emotional body and they held me strongly as I sobbed there for a while. My breathing changed, my tears stopped, and I listened to their message. They said that he was a human whom I had to let go of—he and I had very different paths. They described him as having bad "juju." While "juju" is not really a descriptive term I use, I understood clearly what the trees were saying. In my heart, I knew the message was right, and I began the inner work I needed to do to move on.

This day is one to recommit to your own individual spiritual path. You can initiate those whom you teach or are responsible for through prayer, blessings, ritual, meditation, and journeying. This is a day to create peace and beauty. Create some art while listening to soothing music. Take a walk in nature or a luxurious bath. Reconnect to your own spiritual essence and to the divine. Make some alone time, but do not neglect the wonderful experience of meeting together with others for having rituals. Whether done alone or within a group setting, these are powerful ways to reconnect with the mystery. If you take the time, you will be renewed.

Oir: Spindle

Description: This is a tree of hard wood, commonly used in hedge-rows and often found in coastal areas because it has a tolerance for salty air. Spindle is a delicate, small tree with smooth, gray bark. It has tiny white flowers in June and bright red, deeply lobed fruits on slender stems in autumn.

Ogham: Oir, Oi, Th: ◇
Fulfillment, sweetness and delight
The helmet ogham represents the spindle, formed by the index fingers and thumbs touching at their tips. This tree represents sweetness, delight, and sudden intelligence. It offers inner knowing.

Spindle has a dual nature, sometimes called "thunder and lightning" and is reflected in this ogham's other name, Tharan. It represents sudden flashes of insight and brings illumination and enlightenment.

This tree also promises the fulfillment which comes after the completion of tasks as you walk upon your spiritual journey. Avoid evasion, denial, and excuses. In other words, get to work! Stop talking about what you're going to do, and do it. Fulfillment comes from knowing that you have done your very best. Finish obligations and tasks in your life so you can move forward. This tree's color is white.

Class: Peasant

Rune: Thurisa, Thurisaz ᚦ
Gateway, place of non-action, the god Thor
It is not a time to make decisions; deep transformational forces are at work. Before you make your next move, review and reevaluate. There is still work to be done inside and outside of yourself. Thisrune reminds me of the retrograde periods of Mercury—wonderful times for completion and reevaluation. When you are finally ready to take your next step, be willing to let go of the past. You will be rewarded for your accomplishments. Fulfillment after hard work.

Totems: Thunder beings; Thunderbird; Light beings; Lugh and Lucina; Thor; the Tower card in the tarot in the form of awakening; the three fates; any spinning and weaving goddess such as Spider Woman, Neith, or Isis; Athena, who was credited for inventing weaving as well as all fine arts

Healing

When you have a load of work before you, call on Spindle to help you set your priorities and begin moving step by step. Spindle will keep you focused and productive. Now is not the time to be lazy or avoid what you must do. Step up to the plate and begin. She promises much reward and happiness, because you have worked hard and have earned every bit of your success. She will help you through to completion.

Spindle is a tree that encourages justice and repayment on a karmic level. Keep to the higher road, and even though it may not be immediately evident, the rewards will be great. Be aware that all will reap their own harvest. Those who put attention towards the good may find that the road is longer, but the results will be endearing. Keep to your own business and the universe will take care of the rest. When you forget this fact and get overly involved in other people's stories, ask Spindle to remind you that your only job is your own affairs, intentions, words, and energy.

Spindle energy can be used when you want to bring people together in community. As you bring people together, associate your work with the weaving of a special purpose. In the same way, old stories can be unraveled and rewoven. Take a pattern and tear it apart. Begin anew and take the energy and reweave it into something beautiful with the energy of Spindle.

The Goddess will inspire you with poetry, inner work, divination, and art. Call upon her at the beginning of a quest or if you seek insight into a thorny problem or roadblock.

Uilleand: Honeysuckle

Description: Honeysuckle is a hardy climbing plant. It has dark green, oval leaves that are usually smooth and grow opposite each other in pairs. The branches usually produce many fragrant, trumpet-shaped flowers. These blossoms can range from white, yellow, and pink to purple and scarlet. When the petals drop, little berries form that are a favorite for birds. These plants live a long time. They attract hummingbirds and bees. The white flowers attract sphinx moths at night.

Ogham: Uilleand ("ULL-enth"), the "ui" vowel combination and the "p" and "pe-" consonant combinations: ⚔
Seeking, hidden secrets
The ogham of bones, formed by crossing the index fingers of each hand, represents honeysuckle and instructs us to proceed with caution. This twisting woodbine represents the journey into the self and shows the way in which to connect with inner knowledge, which then helps us discriminate what is worthy from what is of little value. Honeysuckle offers guidance that leads to one's own center. Follow the sweet fragrance of the heart's path; this vine helps one ignore distraction and continue upon the path of spiritual enlightenment. Ivy is concerned with the search for self, and honeysuckle shows us a pattern to follow to achieve this. It serves as a lantern to light the path. Honeysuckle brings assurance that we will find our own hidden soul secrets and discover what has been hidden. Healing is promised after discovery. Light is shed upon the darkness. Its color is light yellow.

Class: Peasant

Rune: Wanjo ᚹ
Joy, light
Rejoice, blessings after the difficulty, new energy, illumination, new clarity, restoration, and alignment

Totems: The lapwing or peewit, hummingbirds, moths, bees, the labyrinth, DNA, the crone or Hermit of the tarot who holds the lantern as you proceed into the dark.

Healing

We often find ourselves distracted, unable to focus, and sense that we have lost our way on the path. Ask Honeysuckle to help you regain your focus and ignore distractions. She will help you to align yourself with what is of real worth and usefulness on your spiritual journey as you move closer and closer to your center. She helps to cut down on the background noise so you can place your efforts towards your own inner knowing.

All of us revisit our wounds from time to time. Honeysuckle reminds us that with each turn of her vine growing towards the light is an opportunity for healing and release. It may feel like opening the same wounds over and over again, but the truth is that you can choose to approach issues from a higher perspective.

At times, we all have a need for camouflage or distraction as a means of establishing protection. The lapwing will fly away from its nest and, by making a unique cry, will draw attention away from its precious eggs and nest. Sometimes we too are reminded that there are people from whom and places from which it is best to hide our light under the bush. It is not always necessary to announce you are a healer or a wisdom keeper; sometimes, it's necessary to protect our most valuable secrets or knowledge. The lapwing also teaches us that the treasure is not to be found in the flight away from the nest. The place of the precious jewel or egg is at the beginning point, the center.

Honeysuckle is all about secrets. It often takes a great deal of circumspection and discipline to keep a secret. Personal secrets full of remorse, shame, and harm will eventually need to be shared in a safe place and with a safe person. The act of holding them in can cause more damage, inflammation, and infection within your soul. In contrast, holding someone's secret can be a sacred act. Although it can be tempting to gossip or use information against someone, it is a sacred act to choose not to. Then there are the secrets of wisdom, light, and higher consciousness which we can find when we do inner work, pay attention to our dreams and visions, take guided meditations, study with a spiritual teacher, or develop our psychic abilities through our efforts with sacred tools. This plant will serve you in your work with secrets.

Honeysuckle is used for essential oil and incense. Its fragrance attracts prosperity and psychic awareness. When you seek privacy, imagine yourself in a beautiful little garden, with a wall of honeysuckle vines growing all around you. Take a moment to smell the lovely scent and breathe in the protection and solitude.

When you are seriously ready to discover your true purpose, take a period of time to sit with the energy of this plant. Listen for her messages. She has revelations to share and will bring insight into your true nature.

Phagos: Beech

Description: Beech is a forest tree. It has thin, papery leaves that turn gold in the fall. The twigs are slender and have spear-shaped buds at their tips. The male flowers are formed in globe-shaped heads and the females are in short, erect spikes. Male and female flowers are separate. A prickly nutcase covers the triangular-shaped beechnuts. The tree's trunk has smooth gray bark. It has well balanced spreading branches.

Ogham: Phagos ("FAH-gus"), "io" vowel combination and "ph" consonant combination: 

Ancient knowledge, generations

The ogham is "the hook." The word "beech" and "book" have the same origins. Ancient knowledge is revealed through old objects, places, and writings. You may feel motivated to do research and study. You may be drawn to mythology, the study of the world religions, philosophy, archeology, or anthropology. You may be drawn to certain cultures and places. The guidance from the past can help with insight and provide solid foundations. Lost wisdom is often the most relevant for modern times. Upon such wisdom, new ideas and interpretations can offer sustenance and guidance. The wisdom could also refer to advice from any elderly person, ancient sources, or your ancestry and lineages; it can be used to make necessary improvements and changes. New experiences and information are coming.

Beech is called "the mother of the woods" and is queen to the king Oak. She provides strong grounding and holds space for smaller trees, humans, and wildlife. Her color is orange-brown. The tree can be used to produce paper, and beechnuts are food for humans and animals. Give Beech gratitude for its giveaway. It is good for carving, but please don't carve your initials on a tree. If you have done so in the past, you are encouraged to make amends. This tree does not tolerate our pollution very well, yet beech groves are powerful places. Divining rods can be made from its wood, and it is a good conductor of electricity.

Class: Chieftain

Rune: Jera   ⟨⟩

Harvest, fertile season, one year

Beneficial outcomes of activity or endeavors to which you are committed. Be advised that it may be a while before results can be reaped. A full cycle must be lived through. Cultivate your project with care. You are offered encouragement and success. Remain patient and work hard and diligently. Honor the process.

Totems: Keys, ancient texts or spell books, the snake, the Great Mother Goddess, the crones, the ancestors, archangels, Merlin, Thoth

Healing

Bark, leaves, roots, and sap have been used for burns, ulcers, bladder and liver problems, and tuberculosis. The bark and leaves have been used for their astringent properties. You can apply beech to these ailments energetically.

Beechnuts can be made into amulets for wisdom. When you handle an old object, read old writing, and visit old places, ask Beech to connect you to the deep knowledge held within. Guidance from the past can help you gain insight into the present and future.

When you begin a new project or endeavor, you need a solid foundation. Sit with a beech tree or imagine one and be with its energy. Ask specifically for a strong foundation on which your project or plan can be built.

Beech may give you a gift of an old book or other resource that supplies you with just the information you need. When you handle an old object, you may be surprised when you gain an understanding of past people or events, and you might even be given a view into a memory associated with the object. Older people may show up to share their life stories, or their understanding and experience. You may be offered a gift of wisdom at just the right moment, and it may help you avoid mistakes otherwise made out of ignorance or a lack of attention. Be open to how Beech's wisdom can be shown to you.

One night, I had a dream that I went to a party and was badly beaten and raped. It was a gruesome dream experience. The next evening I was picked up to go to a party, and it was as if I walked into the exact ambience of the dream! I declined to go to the party and found out later there was a heavy use of drugs, which indeed could have led to the experience within my dream. I'm glad I followed the advice. So often, my dreams have been like a wise fairy godmother or wise old man. They inform me and protect me.

Call in the energy of Beech when you require strength, a strong foundation, and stability. Calling in Beech at Samhain makes contact with ancestors easier and also invites in their wisdom and knowledge.

This tree has worked closely with me. In my study of the Celtic tree calendar, she has been a constant friend, feeding me with books, people, coincidences, journeys, and dreams that encourage and enlighten me. She has been very involved in keeping me to the task of completing the manuscript for this book and getting it to the publisher. She is full of the ancient British peoples' teachings. She is quite happy to see that the work of so many years of my life can be shared.

Mor: The Sea

Description: The ocean, the sea, the rivers and lakes and pools, the saline solution of our own bodies

Ogham: Mor ("mohr"), "ae" vowel combination and "xi" and "x" consonant combinations:

Journey

The ogham of the warp and weft of a shirt represent the sea. The sea represents hidden knowledge. Water represents the moon, lunar aspects, and the feminine principle. The sea is linked with your place of birth and the lands from which you herald. This also represents places you may have to travel to enhance and support your spiritual journey. The sea connects you to the maternal line of your ancestry. All life comes from our mothers and the great mother aspect of nature. Gratitude for life. The color is blue-green.

Class: None

Rune: Eihwaz

Defense, patience

Difficulties may arise at the beginning of a new life or project. Consider that a delay may prove beneficial, and for now, do not push ahead. Perseverance and foresight are needed before you act. Gently mother your project. Avoid stressful conditions. Once clarity is reached, you may move ahead with grace and ease. The universe supports you. Growth is promoted, although you may have to contend with some inconvenience and discomfort. Set your house in order and be diligent.

Totems: Water nymphs and fairies; the keepers of the rivers, streams, wells and pools; rain; the moon goddess; gods and goddesses of your home land; female lineages; Manannán mac Lir, god of the sea; the crane bag

Healing

When you are looking to establish a new home or move to a new place, call in the energy of Mor. When you feel that you are in the hands of destiny, call upon the protection of Mor and all her guides and guardians to promote a good outcome.

Make your own crane bag. In a small pouch, place personal items you spend time and making relationships with. These can be stones, pieces of shells, a pine cone or small stick, and/or a feather. Make sure you talk to each and ask them if they will hold personal space for you. These are not to be used for other people; they are your own personal medicine, used to connect you to source energy and for alignment to your own spiritual essence. Spend time with these helpers after a demanding day and especially when you have channeled healing energy for another. They will restore you.

Mor links you to your place of birth and the lands you may have to travel to on your spiritual passage. She supports actual and astral travel.

When handling family heirlooms or looking through family records and papers, invite Mor and you may receive hidden information or knowledge through messages, images, and synchronicities.

Bring in the power of Mor when you have issues with your mother, daughters, sisters, and other female relatives. Mor represents the great mother and she can help support you emotionally through any difficulty.

Mor represents the unconscious. We all are faced with our shadow and the shadow of others. We are often mystified by our own behaviors and have no conscious explanation for what is driving us or why. We must descend into this unknown territory and bring light to that which is hidden. This is a spiritual pursuit, the process of which is often initiated by a significantly negative experience. Therapy and self-help books can support us in this essential process. I think working with a trusted guide is invaluable, but I also believe personal exploration and solitary inner work is necessary. The teachings shared within this book have been my process for becoming friends with my shadow and for retrieving my own gold out of the darkness. Mor has been my magical cauldron of death, rebirth, and healing.

The Goddess is keeper of the cauldron. Place your questions and concerns into her cauldron and expect the guidance and light that you require. She knows your fears and she is happy to cook them into a new stew. Do not be afraid to be with the ocean. She is you.

APPENDIX B
The Twenty-Five Ogham Letters, Trees, and Runes Chart

The Feada

#	LETTER/ OGHAM	TREE/ MEANING	RUNE/ MEANING
	Aicme Beith		
1	⊢ B/ Beith	Birch/ Beginning	ᛒ Berkano/Growth
2	⊨ L/ Luis	Rowan/ Protection	ᛚ Laguz/Flow
3	⊫ F, V, GW/ Fearn	Alder/ Guidance	ᚠ Fehu/Possessions
4	⊨ S/ Saille	Willow/ Feminine Principle	ᛋ Sowelo/Wholeness
5	⊫ N/ Nuin	Ash/ World Tree	ᚾ Naudhiz/Constraint

#	LETTER/ OGHAM	TREE/ MEANING	RUNE/ MEANING
		Aicme hÚathe	
6	ᚆ H / Huathe	Hawthorn/ Cleansing	ᚺ Hagalaz/Disruption
7	ᚇ D/ Duir	Oak/ Strength	ᛞ Daguz/ Breakthrough
8	ᚈ T/ Tinne	Holly/ Justice	ᛏ Tiwaz/Warrior
9	ᚉ C/ Coll	Hazel/ Intuition	ᚲ Kaunaz/Opening
10	ᚊ Q/ Quert	Apple/ Choice	ᛈ Perth/Initiation
		Aicme Muin	
11	ᚋ M/ Muin	Vine/ Prophecy	ᛗ Mannaz/The Self
12	ᚌ G/ Gort	Ivy/ Labyrinth	ᚷ Gebo/Partnership
13	ᚍ Ng/ Ngetal	Reed/ Direct Action	ᛝ Ingwaz/Fertility
14	ᚎ SS, ST, Z/ Straif	Blackthorn/ Negation	ᛉ Algiz/Protection
15	ᚏ R/ Ruis	Elder/ Renewal	ᚱ Raido/Journey

#	LETTER/ OGHAM	TREE/ MEANING	RUNE/ MEANING
	Aicme Ailim (Vowels)		
16	A / Ailim	Silver Fir/ Foresight	Anzus/ Signals, Messages
17	O/ Ohn	Gorse/Furze/ Collecting	Othila/Separation
18	U, W/ Ur	Heather/Mistletoe/ Healing	Uraz/Strength
19	E/ Eadha	White Poplar/Aspen/ Adversity	Ehwaz/Movement
20	I, J, Y/ Ioho	Yew/ Rebirth	Isa/Standstill

The Forfeda

#	LETTER/ OGHAM	TREE/ MEANING	RUNE/ MEANING
21	EA, CH, KH/ Koad (Shears)	The Grove/ Temple Silence, Intuition	The Blank Rune/ Odin's Rune/ Unknowable
22	OI, TH/ Oir (Helmet)	Spindle/ Fulfillment	Thurisa/ TH: Gateway
23	UI, PE, P/ Uilleand (Bones)	Honeysuckle/ Seeking	Wanjo/ W: Joy

#	LETTER/ OGHAM	TREE/ MEANING	RUNE/ MEANING
24	 IO, PH/ Phagos (Hook)	Beech/ Generations	 Jera/J: Harvest
25	 AE, XI, X/ Mor (Weft of the shirt)	The Sea/ Journey, Maternal Links	 Eihwaz/Ei: Defense

APPENDIX C

The Celtic Wheel of the Year and the Thirteen Moons

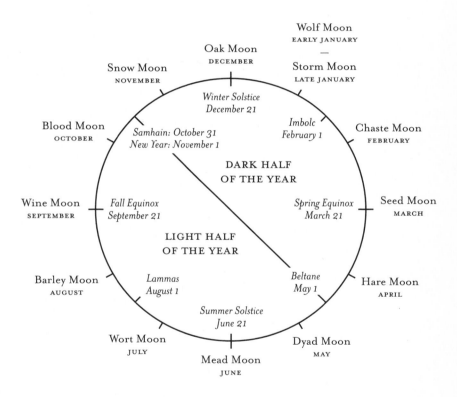

Wolf Moon
EARLY JANUARY
—
Storm Moon
LATE JANUARY

Oak Moon
DECEMBER

Snow Moon
NOVEMBER

Winter Solstice
December 21

Imbolc
February 1

Chaste Moon
FEBRUARY

Blood Moon
OCTOBER

Samhain: October 31
New Year: November 1

DARK HALF
OF THE YEAR

Wine Moon
SEPTEMBER

Fall Equinox
September 21

Spring Equinox
March 21

Seed Moon
MARCH

LIGHT HALF
OF THE YEAR

Barley Moon
AUGUST

Lammas
August 1

Beltane
May 1

Hare Moon
APRIL

Wort Moon
JULY

Summer Solstice
June 21

Dyad Moon
MAY

Mead Moon
JUNE

APPENDIX D
Celtic Holidays and Celebrations

NOVEMBER 1	Celtic New Year, Day of the Dead
DECEMBER 21–22	Winter Solstice, Yule
FEBRUARY 1–2	Imbolc, Imbolg, Candlemas, Brigantia
MARCH 21	Vernal Equinox, Alban Eiler, Easter, Eostre, Ostara
MAY 1	Beltane, May Day
JUNE 21	Summer Solstice, Alban Heruin, Midsummer
AUGUST 1	Lammas, Festival of the Bread, Lughnasa, Lughnassad
SEPTEMBER 21–22	Autumnal Equinox, Alban Elved, Mabon, the Harvest
OCTOBER 31	Samhain, Halloween, Hallowmas, The Day

The Holidays

The holidays are known as the eight "spokes" of the Wheel of the Year. Ancient wisdom teaches that it is essential to pay attention to and honor nature's time cycles. Ritual and ceremony were believed to ensure right order and the continuance of life. Keeping to these sun and moon celebrations were part of proper respect and stewardship. It was also believed that an opening in the crack between the worlds was created at each of these special times of the year, and that it was possible at that time to connect and communicate with the spirit realms. This connection allowed for inspiration, guidance, and renewal. It was a wonderful thing for humans to have open communication with the magical, mystical, and enchanted. While this kind of contact can never be fully explained, it offers sparks of creativity, insight, inspiration, and joy. Bliss and ecstasy are good for us. See if you can make some time on each of these holidays to connect with the spiritual realm.

November 1: The Celtic New Year, the Day of the Dead, Nos Galan Gaeaf

This holiday occurs at the end of the Elder month and the beginning of the Birch month. The Celtic New Year overlaps with Samhain and begins the dark half of the year. Beginning on the sunset of October 31, this is a time to confront our troubles and settle accounts. We are encouraged to let go of that which cannot be sufficiently resolved, leaving it to the higher powers to determine outcomes and karma. Now is the time to throw out old ideas and influences to prepare for new beginnings. Clean the slate of the past year and set new intentions. That which has not come to fruition can be recycled so energy can be used to create new ideas, plans, and strategies.

This was also a time to give gratitude and for making contact with spirits, ancestors and the "group mind" of the clan (Murphy, 111). We honor the crone who has authority over death and rebirth. In the Celtic tradition, we honor Cerridwen, Tara, Holle, the Hag, the Cailleach, and the Morrigan and their totem, the sow. The white sow was a favorite animal for the crone to shapeshift into.

We also honor our grandmothers, maternal lineages, and our ancestors. We invite the dead to dinner, and recognize they have helpful things to share. We make space to listen to their messages. We often make altars with pictures and objects that belonged to our beloved departed ones. We celebrate death and rebirth, and recognize that "passing over" is but another door opening to another realm. Baba Ram Dass equates this experience with that of taking off a tight shoe.

December 21–22: Winter Solstice, Alban Arthuan, Midwinter, Yule

This holiday occurs at the end of the Luis/Rowan month and we honor the tall evergreen trees that represent the ogham Ailim and all firs, spruces, and cedars. This time marks the shortest day of the year and the longest night. This is a solar celebration that marks the rebirth of the goddess/god and the return of the sun, the light, and the promise of spring, when food may again be planted, grown, and replenished. Here we honor the element of earth and the direction of north. North represents the dark, winter, midnight, wisdom, the ancients, and the ancestors. It also represents the wisdom of our own bodies as wonderful houses for our spirits.

For our ancestors, winter celebrations were an essential part of survival. Honoring the spirits in nature as well as the deities that supported their lives was a crucial aspect of life. The candles and bonfires of this time brought light to the darkness and helped our ancestors keep their hope alive as they endured another winter, often a time of starvation and illness. The solstice is a good time for us to rest in darkness and let ideas germinate, like animal hibernation or gestation within the womb. It is a good time for quiet, inner work, and contemplation. The modern association of this season as one where people go into shopping and spending frenzies is an interesting one—we're really going against the natural energy!

Honoring the longest night of the year also meant celebrating the birth of the new sun. Originally the birth of the sun was seen as female. The goddesses of Yule are Persephone or Kore of Greece, Rhiannon of Wales, Gráinne of Ireland, Graine of Scotland, and Isis and Hathor of Egypt. As cultures became patriarchal, the men become more prominent. Many cultures around the planet chose December 25 for the birthdate of these special men of power, healing, and enlightenment who brought hope to the world. Some of these leaders were Jesus, Mithra, Saturn, Dionysus, Tammuz, Quetzacoatl, Adonis, Attis, Frey, Osiris, Horus, Buddha, and Herne the Hunter.

We would do well to remember that these special sons were born of flesh and blood to special women. Because Celtic tradition honors the creative magic and mystery of the maiden, mother, and crone, we remember that all these great sons/suns are gifts from the mother/Gaia. Thus we honor Mother Mary, Mab, Modron, and many others. All these births represent the movement from the barren of winter towards the hope of spring. We celebrate the mystery of conception, gestation, and birth.

February 1–2: Imbolc, Imbolg, Immolc, Oimelc, Candlemas

This holiday falls in the middle of the Saille/Willow month with its lunar and female associations. This is a moon celebration falling six weeks after the solstice. It is a fire festival that welcomes the sun. Lighting fires and candles brings light and warmth into the darkness and cold, representing the spark of new life or the beginning of the growth of the seed underground. The crescent moon and the maiden aspect of the Goddess are honored at this time. While we are reminded of fire, let us envision the "zap" of magic that causes seeds to grow. We also honor the hearth fires and the sacred fire within. Within ourselves is a holy shrine, and it is our responsibility to keep it burning. This is the time of year for initiations, inspiration, and new plans.

Imbolc represents the womb or spring time and stands for the milk of the pregnant ewe. "Imbolc" itself literally translates to "in the belly." We note that it takes nine months within the womb for a child to develop. Now is the time to honor the child growing within the pregnant mother. We look forward not only to springtime but to the births of the children conceived from sacred unions of the light half of the year.

This holiday is especially sacred to the triple fire goddess Brigit. She is of multiples forms—as maid, mother, and the old hag—and is the goddess of poetry, healing, creativity, healing, and smith craft. She is the muse of inspiration and the patroness of childbirth and prosperity. She has three talismans: the shining mirror (allows entrance into other worlds and is used for scrying), the spinning wheel (creation), and the grail or cauldron of rebirth. She is associated with the white swan, the cow, the wolf, the snake, and all birds of prey, as well as the archangel Michael. She is associated with the Isle of Avalon and it is interesting to note that the outline of a swan in flight is formed by the contours of the hills of Somerset, believed to be the present-day location of this mystic isle.

March 21: The Vernal Equinox, Alban Eiler, Easter, Ostara

This celebration begins the Hawthorn month. Within this sun holiday we honor the east and the beginning of spring. We again return to a portal of equal day and equal night in the waxing cycle of the year, and honor the maiden aspect of the mother and the rebirth of the earth. The word "easter" comes from the Saxon fertility goddess Ostara. Other spellings of this goddess's name are Eaostre, Eostre, or Oestre. The hare and the egg are sacred symbols of this regenerative power.

Ostara is a time to celebrate the fertility of nature. Buds and branches begin to grow. We celebrate the stage of growth of our children as they become young men and woman, honoring their sexual awakening. Early flowers and new shoots bless us, and the birds return with their songs and nest building. We celebrate the fact that we have made it through winter and prepare soil for planting. Now is also the time for cleansing and purification—of making ready. Spring cleaning is on our minds, as is letting go of what no longer nourishes us. This is the time when young bucks show themselves and begin to grow their great antlers. Ohn Gorse is a bush to use during this celebration.

Ritual at this time is dedicated to this annual warming of the earth and the renewal of her fertility as seeds begin to sprout after a long hibernation. This is a good time of year for initiations, making wishes for the renewal of hope, creativity, wisdom, success in a project, or better relationships. Such wishes can be hopes and dreams for ourselves, or they can be for others as well. This time of year is good for making vows. Expectation, and possibilities are ripe in this festival of freshness. This time marks the end of the dark half of the year.

May 1: Beltain, Beltane, May Day

This is a moon holiday that begins the light half of the year, falling within the Oak month. This is the feast day of the god Belenos, who protected cattle with his sacred fires and was the guardian of medicinal herbs. As a consort of the Great Mother, he represented fire and fertility. He is known as the Green Man or Pan. This is the sexiest of the holidays—it is said that men and women copulated in the fields to ensure a bountiful harvest. Eroticism was embraced as the heart of fertility and the celebration of life, and there was no shame or embarrassment attached to sensuality. Children born of these unions were sacred to the community, gifts of the Goddess who encouraged pleasure and sensual delights.

Beltane is the festival of the Maypole dance. The white ribbons of the maypole represent semen and the red ribbons the menstrual cycle. The dance represents the sexual act and the insemination of the womb. Jumping over a bonfire is done to foster positive fertile energy. Driving livestock between two bonfires was believed to ensure their fertility, as well as kill off harmful parasites. Flowers and garlands are placed in May baskets and given away. We honor the maiden aspect of the Goddess here as she prepares for her first sexual experiences.

This holiday signifies the beginning of summer in the old European growing season, the time for sowing seeds. Ritual's purpose was to ensure a healthy crop and a bountiful harvest in the late summer and fall. This is the time of year to honor the faeries and the little people. We give gratitude to the devas and dryads of each plant and tree species who organize and protect every aspect of their seasonal growth. This is a special time of magic and gaiety; frolic and merriment.

June 21: Summer Solstice, Alban Heruin, Midsummer, Litha

This holiday falls in the middle of the Coll/Hazel month. Here we celebrate the longest day of the year and the shortest night. The sun has reached its peak and fullness and from this day on, the days will become shorter. We honor the sun gods and goddesses. The goddess of midsummer is the mother aspect of the Goddess. She represents abundance, fertility, and power, and we celebrate these attributes at this time. Ur/Heather and Mistletoe can be used to celebrate this particular holiday.

We honor the goddesses of beauty and mature sexuality. They are Gaia, Aphrodite, Corn Mother, Hera, Demeter, and Rhiannon. At this juncture, Herne the Hunter shows himself and begins his journey to find the great stag.

On this holiday, people jumped bonfires and made midsummer bonfire wishes. You can use a candle to do this, or a small (contained!) outdoor fire. It's great fun to jump over the fire while saying your wishes out loud. For example, you could say, "I claim a successful business. I claim a beautiful house!" We honor the people in our lives revered as heroes and heroines. This is a time for drums, dance, and song. We give blessings for abundance, crops, and fruits growing in the fields and orchards.

August 1: Lammas, Lughnasa, The Day of the Bread, The Festival of the Bread

Lammas is a celebration of the first fruits of the harvest. Here is where the hopes, wishes, and seeds planted six months ago begin to come to fruition. This is the time when marriages took place, legal proceedings were dealt with, and contests and sporting events took place.

Lammas is a fire holiday and a festival for Lugh (sometimes spelled Lleu or Lu). He is the god of light that represents the full power of the sun. He is responsible for the first rewards of harvest. The growing seeds begin to share their fruit, and it is a time of plenty. With the grain, the corn, and the grape, humans begin to receive the light of the sun into their bodies. Lammas was very important as a festival to honor and show gratitude. Without it, there was no guarantee of another year of survival for the community as it braced itself for autumn and winter. The seeds were honored and then stored for another planting season.

The Goddess and God were united in a sexual dance of the sacred marriage. Rites were practiced that ritualistically took the life of the son/lover/stag/grain/crop. There was no human sacrifice; instead, this was more like a theatrical experience or re-enactment. The seed would be carried in the womb of the great mother (or the representative of the Goddess), so that new life could occur in another cycle of seasons. Seeds were gathered and saved in sacred vessels so they could birth in the spring when the return of the sun would allow them to sprout.

September 21–22: Autumnal Equinox, Alban Elved, Mabon, Harvest Festival

This arrives in the middle of the Ngetal/Reed month. The Eadha poplar is a tree that can be used in any ceremony that marks this time of year. Again we come to equal day and night as we prepare for winter. Thus begins the season of death. Lugh and Lucina bid us their farewell. This is the time of the final harvest and gratitude is an important part of this holiday, an early Thanksgiving celebration.

We gather the last of the harvest and store seeds and food for the winter. We gather in our fruits and vegetables from our gardens. Leaves begin to falls from trees in earnest, blown loose by the increasing winds and change in the weather. Now is the time to gather herbs, seeds, and leaves to add to our crane bags and medicine supplies. Mabon is a time of repose and resting after the labors of planting and harvesting. We compost, mulch, recycle, and review in preparation for the winter. This is a time to turn inwardly and let go of that which has not born fruit in our personal lives.

Demeter must let go of her Persephone as she descends into the underworld. Herne hunts down the stag and becomes the god Cernunnos. The stag gives up its life for the people. The corn and wheat are ground into flour. Soon the stag will die as well. He will take off his crown of antlers and return them to the earth.

October 31: Halloween, Hallomas, Samhain

Samhain is called *The Day* and is the most important celebration of the year. This holiday actually begins at sunset on October 30 and extends into the Celtic New Year, which begins at sunset on October 31. It marks the beginning of the dark half of the year, in which marriage was forbidden. Its meaning are endings and beginnings, and death and rebirth. This is a time when the veil between the worlds is very thin. Protection was set in place to ward off harmful or mischievous spirits, and communication with the dead and the spirit world was encouraged. This was a time to honor one's ancestors and those who had passed over. Samhain was dedicated to the ghosts of all generations of ancestors during a time when worship of ancestors was the basis of tribal bonding. Each ghost was invited to the feast as a guest. And after being fed and entertained, the ghosts might offer oracular guidance to the living descendants. The Ioho/Yew tree is important to this holiday, as is the Koad rune, standing for the grove.

This is a celebration of the hags and crones who embrace wisdom and death, destruction and renewal. As the third aspect of the Goddess the hag or the crone was known as an avenger, destroyer, and protector. Some of these crones are Kali, Baba Yaga, Cerridwen, Kelle, the Cailleach, Lilith, and Holle. Samhain is also the time for remembering the millions of women who were mutilated, tortured, burned, drowned, stoned, and hung during the Inquisition and witch hunts throughout Europe and North America. This is the time of year to honor all people who are oppressed and struggling for freedom. This is also a good time of year to give your time or money to a cause that supports those who are downtrodden or fighting for their economic, political, religious, or civil rights.

Samhain was also a time to compost the old and save that which was worthwhile—the seeds for the coming year's promise. This is a time of purification and self-reflection and a time to draw life deeply into our own center. Go within, commune with your particular totems, guides, and deities, and make sacred time for meditation and reflection. Now is the time for scrying, trance, prophecies, automatic writing, and crystal-ball gazing. Use your divination tools. Seek communication with the dead. Serve them a plate of food at the table. Build altars for them. Remember your pets who have passed on. This is a good time for festivals and for costumes and masks. Seek places that are sacred to you. Let the dead teach you that no one ever really dies.

APPENDIX E

Calling the Directions

I call the East, the rising sun, and springtime. I call new beginnings and new ideas. I call the winged ones. I call a higher perspective to all our endeavors. I call the element of air and I honor the four winds. I honor intelligence, inspiration, and communication. I honor the trees of the east and its deities, totems, guides, and guardians.

I call the South, the midday sun, and summer. I call fertility and creativity, passion, and activity. I call the plants, flowers, and trees. I call the element of fire and honor our passions, sexuality, and desires. I honor purpose and will, action and creative endeavor. I honor the trees of the south and its deities, totems, guides, and guardians.

I call the West, the setting sun, and autumn. I call the dreamtime and inner reflection. I call all water creatures. I call the element of water and I honor all the waters of the Earth. I honor our tears, emotions, and feelings. I honor flow and receptivity. I honor the trees of the west and its deities, totems, guides, and guardians.

I call the North. I call the midnight sun and winter. I call the wisdom of the ancestors and the knowledge of our lineages. I call the element of earth and I honor our bodies that house our spirits. I honor rocks, minerals, crystals and gems, mountains and valleys, prairies and fields, and deserts. I honor two-legged animals and four-legged animals. I honor the trees of the north and its deities, totems, guides, and guardians.

I call Above. I call the star nations, higher dimensions of consciousness, and love. I call the gods, goddesses, and the angelic realm that participates one hundred percent in love and protection for all.

I call Below. I call Mother Earth and give great gratitude for all she does to sustain our lives. I give great gratitude for all creatures and the unseen domains that nourish us. Without her permission, there would be no flora or fauna to sustain us. She is a paradise and it is a privilege to walk upon her.

I call Within. I honor our heart's altar and feed the flame of love. From this inner place we receive everything we need to know. This is the home of our own inner world tree and our knowledge and love. The heart is the true master organ, where our true eyes and ears are. This is our master message center that connects us to all that is: past, present, and future. This is the place outside time and space, and the emptiness within which all potential and possibility rests. And so it is!

A Celtic Tree Ceremony

Ceremonies can be done for every month marked by a special tree in the Celtic calendar. Other important times to do ceremony are at the equinoxes and solstices, which mark the changing of the seasons, honoring the sun. The cross-quarter holidays honor the moon and fall six weeks between an equinox and a solstice. You might also wish to include ceremony at the new moon and full moon. Once you establish a rhythm in using these ceremonies, you can experiences first-hand the power and teachings revealed and given to you in this book.

As I work with a tree, I go and ask for leaves, branches, berries, twigs, or the fruit of the tree I am honoring. I have found the trees to be very happy to be asked, and they have always been generous in allowing me a sample of their essence. You can also find pictures of the trees in books, in magazines, and on the Internet. Collect poems and stories about trees you like.

Preparation

Once I have decided upon my ceremony and the date and time, I invite my friends to come. If I find they are unable to join me, I do my ceremony alone. Create a central altar on which you can place special objects. Have your participants bring things as well. You might include flowers and tree items that you have collected. I also include little statues and pictures of the particular totems, guides, and deities associated with my particular purpose. Gems and stones also like to be included.

Casting the Circle

When we come together and sit in a circle, I light a central candle and I call the directions beginning with the east, then the south, the west, and finally the north. I call Father Sky above and all the star and thunder beings. I call Mother Earth below me and give her gratitude for sustaining our lives. I call the center within, asking each person to place their hands upon their heart, the cauldron of mystery, divinity, oneness, and the universal. Cast your circle in whatever manner you feel comfortable, and incorporate whatever you feel is right for your circle. There is no right or wrong way to cast it—even if you cannot go out in nature, you may picture in your head a lovingly decorated altar in a quiet wood.

I also call in the particular tree and its totems, guides, and deities. Sometimes I invoke the energies of the particular holiday or moon phase I am invoking at the time. We often sing, chant, and drum. Allow the energy of the circle to grow. You will feel the particular combination of helpers, sounds, beats, and energies that come through. Let them guide you. The more often you meet with your particular group, the better the drumming and singing becomes. You learn to become one with the music and lose any inhibitions and self-consciousness you might have around using your voice or beating your drum.

Purpose of the Ceremony

I usually have a theme whenever performing a ceremony. Right at the beginning is the time to state the purpose and intentions for your ceremony clearly. For instance, I may be honoring a tree and calling forth its wisdom, or I may be celebrating the Celtic New Year. Or perhaps I am undertaking something new at the new moon, or I am calling forth fulfillment at the full moon. If I am beginning with Birch, I am celebrating the month of November and new beginnings for the new year ahead. We can plant seeds for what we hope to bring into another year of life on the planet. We can thank our relatives and ancestors for their gifts, blessings, desires, and even retroactive teachings. We can let go of things or patterns we no longer want to drag around. Or perhaps New Year's resolutions are the focus—we can ask for support to strengthen our determination for achieving a goal. We can receive messages from the ancestors. If I am planning to include any of these things during the ceremony, I share this with my group.

Teaching

I begin by stating what is important at this particular time of year and what portal and energies are available. I share information about the totems, guides, and deities. This is a short teaching moment.

Guided Meditation

A ceremony is often enhanced by a guided meditation or a shamanic journey.

Body of the Ceremony and Activities

It is during this time that we plant seeds, share with each other, make our wishes known, or perform other activities.

Giving the Energy a Place to Go

We close by giving the energy we have created a place to go. We direct it to an intention implied by the activities and purpose of the ceremony. When celebrating Birch, we can direct the energy we have created to sustain and nurture the seeds that represent what we want to grow. This is also a time to place the names of loved ones into the circle for healing. We invite in healing for our loved ones, our relations, and ourselves. We can direct healing energy to a current world situation or event. We can send peace to a troubled area.

Ending the Ceremony and Opening the Circle

We thank the four cardinal directions. We also give thanks to the above, below, and center. We include the guides, totems, and deities, and allow them to return to their native realms. This part is called releasing the directions. We give our gratitude to the particular tree we worked with. Our gratitude is the most important element in working with the spirit realm and with nature's energies. We honor the particular holiday, marking the special time of the year in the turning of the wheel. We usually then take hands and sing an ending song together. We stand for a few moments in the silence, just to gather the lovely energy and ask that it remain with us until the next time we meet. My suggested songs for ending are:

> May the circle be open, but never broken.
> May the peace of the Goddess be ever in our hearts.
> Merry meet and merry part,
> And merry meet again!

or

> We are a circle, within a circle
> With no beginning and never ending.
> (repeat, can be sung in rounds)

RESOURCES

Links to Organizations Working
to Protect the Trees and Our Environment

Friends of the Earth

www.foe.org

FOE is a national environmental organization dedicated to preserving the health and diversity of the planet for future generations.

Rainforest Action Network

www.ran.org

Described as environmentalism with teeth and campaigns for the forests, its inhabitants and the natural life-sustaining systems by transforming the global marketplace through education.

Rainforest Alliance

www.rainforest-alliance.org

Fights deforestation, addresses climate change, protects forests, supports productive farms, helps to improve communities and clean water, and facilitate healthy habitats.

Ancient Forest International

www.ancientforest.org

The Nature Conservancy

www.nature.org

The Nature Conservancy protects Earth's most important natural places for you and future generations.

American Forests

www.americanforests.org

This nonprofit group works to "protect, restore, and enhance the natural capital of trees and forests."

Arbor Day Foundation

www.arborday.org

Buy trees and give a gift of trees through our Trees in Memory and Trees for America … The Arbor Day Foundation is a 501(c)(3) nonprofit conservation and education organization. Volunteer with a local tree-planting organization.

Circle of Life Foundation

www.circleoflifefoundation.org

Promotes sustainability, restoration, and preservation of life; founded by Julia Butterfly Hill, author of *The Legacy of Luna*.

Trees Foundation

www.treesfoundation.org

Nonprofit organization that works to conserve and preserve forest ecosystems.

The Rainforest Site

www.therainforestsite.com

The Rainforest Site funds preservation of endangered habitat around the world, protecting the Earth and the creatures who live here. Click today and every day to help preserve our land.

Trees for the Future

www.plant-trees.org

Planet Green

http://planetgreen.discovery.com/work-connect/
planet-trees-10-bucks.html

National Audubon Society

www.audubon.org

The mission of the National Audubon Society is to conserve and restore natural ecosystems.

Tree Huggers of America

www.treehuggersofamerica.org

A 501(c)(3) organization

Tree People

www.treepeople.org

TreePeople is an environmental nonprofit that unites the power of trees, people, and technology to grow a sustainable future for Los Angeles.

Save Our Trees

save-our-trees.org

An international nonprofit environmental project to help save trees, paper, and money.

Greenpeace

www.greenpeace.org

Greenpeace is an environmental group that is known the world over. They have grown from a very simple beginning into a global organization.

Trees Are Good

www.treesaregood.com/treecare/treecareinfo.aspx

Tree care information. We note the heroic efforts of individuals and organizations to save particularly large or historic trees in a community.

How to Help Save Trees

www.ehow.com/how_5684175_save-tree_s.html

The following two societies have many educated members that are available to help plan tree preservation and new tree plantings. (Scott Baker, principal of Tree Solutions Inc., is a registered consulting arborist and certified arborist. He recommends an excellent book by Nelda Matheny and James R. Clark, *Trees and Development: A Technical Guide to Preservation of Trees During Land Development*, as a resource to get started in your understanding of tree preservation.)

International Society of Arboriculture

www.isa-arbor.com

The American Society of Consulting Arborists

www.asca-consultants.org

Resources
Organizations and Healers

Carol Marcy, PhD, Hollywood, MD

www.joylanehealingcenter.net

claybasket@verizon.net

Carol is a psychologist and director of the Joy Lane Healing Center, a place where spirit and healing meet, and classes and workshops are given in a variety of healing arts. In her private practice, she uses a variety of energy/spiritual practices combined with more traditional psychological approaches in a partnership for healing. The Center's 62 acres of woodland is held as sacred space, and provides a deeply healing environment. Her book, *Living Life as a Prayer*, helps the reader to consciously create the living prayer that he or she is manifesting by developing an awareness of the thoughts, words, actions, and feelings of everyday life.

Danielle Rama Hoffman, Seattle

www.divinetransmissions.com

www.egyptiscalling.com

Danielle is a healer and teacher of metaphysics. Her areas of focus include the Egyptian Mysteries, Egyptian Mysteries Temple Essences, the Harmonizer Program, Egypt is Calling Tours which takes groups to Egypt, and incredible energy readings. She has authored *The Temples of Light: An Initiatory Journey into the Heart Teachings of the Egyptian Mystery Schools* and also produced twenty Guided Initiations to accompany her book in a six-CD set.

Deanne Duff, Kent, WA

pureessencespa@msn.com

Delightful massage therapist and energy healer.

Dr. Friedemann Schaub, MD, PhD, Seattle

www.cellularwisdom.com

www.egyptiscalling.com

He has developed a personal breakthrough and empowerment program, which uses a unique blend of mind activating technologies such as neuro-linguistic programming (NLP), clinical hypnotherapy, and Time-Line Therapy™ and his medical and scientific expertise. The program is designed to remove emotional and mental blocks from the level of the subconscious mind and cellular memory, thus activating each individual's capacity to heal, change, and succeed in any area of life. This program is especially helpful with anxiety, depression, and chronic pain. Dr. Schaub's work is available worldwide via skype or phone. Friedemann also leads spiritual journeys to Egypt together with his wife, Danielle Rama Hoffman

Gaia's Temple, Seattle

www.gaiastemple.org

This Goddess Temple is founded and led by Rev. Judith Laxer and offers Goddess worship services to the Seattle community. Everyone is welcome.

Gloria Taylor Brown, San Diego, CA

www.Gloriataylorbrown.com

Psychic; shaman; channeler; certified alchemical healer and teacher; businesswoman; and speaker. With Normandi Ellis, she co-authored *Remembering the Divine Within: Writing Your Spiritual Autobiography* and was the primary visionary with Nicki Scully in *Becoming the Oracle*, a series of recorded journeys that will allow you to explore oracles all around the world. She is available by phone and in person for consultations.

Irene Iris Ingalls, Seattle

www.Lightlanguageart.com

Irene@Lightlanguageart.com

Professional visual artist, alchemical healer and energy medicine healer, and intuitive light language scribe. Makes individual language of light art for your healing and empowerment.

Jamie Luce, Mulketeo, WA

estomagic@yahoo.com

Jamie is an esthetician, Reiki Master and alchemical healer. She has a strong connection to the land where she lives and the nature spirits that grace her garden. Jamie conveys a strong sense of grounding and belonging through her energy work.

Jonny Hahn, Seattle

Jonnyhhahn@yahoo.com

Pianist-Singer-Songwriter, has been street performing at the Pike Place Public Market and at assorted fairs and festivals since 1986. He is an amazing energy healer and can work at a distance as well as in person.

Rev. Judith Laxer, Seattle

www.judithlaxer.com

Judith is a minister, spiritual counselor, psychic tarot reader, ceremonialist and hypnotherapist.

Karen Johannsen, MA, Shoreline, WA

ksjohannsen@gmail.com

Karen is a spiritual counselor, Reiki Master, teacher, leader of full moon meditations, guided imagery facilitator, and also practices drumming circles and esoteric astrology.

Kathryn Ravenwood, Albuquerque, NM

kravenwood@yahoo.com

Certified alchemical healer and teacher, tarot card reader, licensed massage therapist, and also works with sound and light therapies. She is a ceremonialist and ordained minister, and offers personal and public rituals. Healing sessions and readings are "telephone friendly!"

Kelly Malone, Seattle

Kelly@thirdandfinal.com

Kelly is involved in writing and editing. She is an author, and loves to work on clients' spiritual writing projects.

Laura Bailey, Seattle

www.samaraskincare.com

Laura is a skincare specialist, manicurist, and energy medicine practitioner. Laura creates a sensory haven that blends cultures, color, and elements in exquisite harmony to calm the mind, soothe the body, and nurture the skin.

Linda Star Wolf, Sylva, NC

www.shamanicbreathwork.org

starwolf@shamanicbreathwork.org

venusrising@shamanicbreathwork.org

Linda is founder and director of the Venus Rising Institute for Shamanic Healing Arts, president of Venus Rising University for Shamanic-

Psycho-Spiritual Degrees, founder of Shamanic Ministers Global Network and Training Program, creator of the Shamanic Breathwork™ process, author of five books, and has contributed to many more. She has been a Shamanic-Psycho-Spiritual Teacher/Facilitator for more than thirty years. Star Wolf teaches how to "Awaken the Shaman Within."

Nicki Scully, Eugene, OR

www.becominganoracle.com

www.theanubisoracle.com

www.hathorsmirror.com

Nicki is a ceremonialist, speaker, and teacher of healing, shamanic arts, and the Egyptian Mysteries. Thousands of practitioners worldwide use her techniques from Alchemical Healing, a comprehensive healing form she developed. Nicki founded Shamanic Journeys, Ltd. in the late eighties and has been guiding inner journeys and spiritual pilgrimages to Egypt and other sacred sites ever since. Nicki's published books include *Alchemical Healing: A Guide to Spiritual, Physical, and Transformational Medicine* and *Power Animal Meditations*, as well as *The Anubis Oracle* and *Shamanic Mysteries of Egypt*, both co-authored with Linda Star Wolf. Her most recent work is *Becoming An Oracle: Connecting with the Divine Source for Information and Healing*, a 7-CD audio program. www.shamanicjourneys.com

Normandi Ellis, Frankfort, KY

www.normandiellis.com

Author, speaker, and workshop leader, and runs a writing center called PenHouse Retreat Center. She leads writing groups to Egypt. She has authored *Awakening Osiris*, *Dreams of Isis*, and *Feasts of Light, Celebrations for the Seasons of Life based on the Egyptian Goddess Mysteries* as well as others.

Ricardo Hidalgo, LMHC, Seattle

Ricardo is a licensed mental health counselor at the University of Washington. He also works as a consultant for agencies who work with Hispanic populations. He helps people navigate out of stress. He uses psychology, philosophy, spiritual teachings, literature, and physics in his practice. He uses his own inner wisdom, which he says is not "his own" but which we all "own" in the sense that we all have a line to "universal wisdom."

Sandy Nisley-Leader, Carmel Valley, CA

sandraknl@aol.com

A Religious Science minister, Sandy Leader uses spiritual mind treatment for healing and life enhancement. She has been teaching spiritual and meditation classes and leading retreats for the past decade. Her great passion and joy is helping others recognize, develop and express their creative potential.

Starfeather, Edmonds, WA

www.shimmeringpath.com

Healer, ceremonialist, spiritual counselor, channeler, visionary artist, and writer. Starfeather considers all her specialties to be aspects of the same journey—that of service to Mother Earth and all our relations. She does vibrational upliftment, healing sessions, and channeled guidance by appointment, in addition to Heart Expansion Ceremonies, and spiritual retreats. She is also a custom drum and shield maker.

Women of Wisdom, Seattle

www.womenofwisdom.org

The Women of Wisdom Foundation is a national women's organization based in Seattle, providing diverse and innovative programs that offer women opportunities for personal growth and transformation.

WOW promotes women's spirituality, creativity, and wholeness, and empowers women's voices and their contributions to the world, honoring the Divine Feminine in all. Women's events include a range of mind, body, and spirit topics for a full healing experience. This foundation runs a yearly conference in Seattle in February and brings in women from all over the country. Founded by Kris Steinnes. Look for her book *Women of Wisdom: Empowering the Dreams and Spirits of Women*, Wise Women Publishing, 2008.

BiBLiOGRAPHY

Andrews, Lynn V. *The Woman of Wyrrd*. New York: Harper Perennial, 1990.

Blum, Ralph H. *The Book of Runes*. New York: St. Martin's Press, 1993.

Budapest, Zsuzsanna Emese.*The Holy Book of Women's Mysteries*. Berkeley, CA: Wingbow Press, 1980.

Chase, Pamela Louise, and Jonathan Pawlik. *Trees for Healing: Harmonizing with Nature for Personal Growth and Planetary Balance*. North Hollywood, CA: Newcastle Publishing Co., 1991.

Conway, D. J. *Celtic Magic*. St. Paul, MN: Llewellyn Publications, 1991.

Cowan, Eliot. *Plant Spirit Medicine*. Columbus, NC: Swan Raven & Company, 1995.

Fleming, Fergus, Shahrukh Husain, Scott C. Littleton, and Linda A. Malcor. *Time-Life Books: Heroes of the Dawn: Celtic Myth*. London: Duncan Baird Publishers, 1996.

Gantz, Jeffrey, trans. *The Mabinogion*. London: Penguin Books, 1976.

Graves, Robert. *The White Goddess*. New York: Farrar, Straus and Giroux, 1948.

Greer, John Michael, and David Spangler. *The Druid Magic Handbook: Ritual Magic Rooted in the Living Earth.* San Francisco: Weiser Books, 2007.

Hartmann, Thom. *The Last Hours of Ancient Sunlight: Waking Up to Personal and Global Transformation.* Northfield, VT: Mythical Books, 1998.

Hill, Julia Butterfly. *The Legacy of Luna: The Story of a Tree, A Woman, and the Struggle to Save the Redwood.* New York: Harper Collins, 2000.

Holmes, Ernest. *The Science of Mind: A Philosophy, A Faith, A Way of Life.* New York: Penguin Putnam, 1938.

Jones, Kathy. *The Ancient British Goddess: Her Myths, Legends and Sacred Sites.* Somerset, UK: Ariadne Publications, 1991.

Kindred, Glennie. *The Sacred Tree.* Derbyshire, UK: Self-Published, 1995.

Kozocari, Jean, Jessica North, and Yvonne Owens. *The Witch's Book of Days.* Victoria, BC: Beach Holme Publishers, 1994.

Kynes, Sandra. *Whispers from the Woods.* Woodbury, MN: Llewellyn Publications, 2006.

Lappé, Frances Moore, and Anna Lappé. *Hope's Edge: The Next Diet for a Small Planet.* New York: Jeremy P. Tarcher/Putnam, 1982.

Leek, Sybil. *A Ring of Magic Islands.* Garden City, NY: American Photographic Book Publishing Co., 1976.

McColman, Carl. *The Complete Idiot's Guide to Celtic Wisdom.* New York: Alphy, a division of Penguin, 2003.

McCoy, Edain. *Celtic Myth and Magick.* St. Paul, MN: Llewellyn Publications, 2002.

———. *Celtic Women's Spirituality: Accessing the Cauldron of Life.* St. Paul, MN: Llewellyn Publications, 1998.

Medicine Eagle, Brooke. *Buffalo Woman Comes Singing.* New York: Ballantine Books, 1991.

Morgan, Ffiona. *Wild Witches Don't Get the Blues: Astrology, Rituals and Healing.* Forestville, CA: Daughters of the Moon Publishing, 1991.

Murray, Colin, and Liz Collins. *The Celtic Tree Oracle: A System of Divination.* New York: St. Martin's Press, 1988.

Noble, Vicki. *Shakti Woman: Feeling Our Fire, Healing Our World.* San Francisco: Harper, 1991.

O'Driscoll, Robert. *The Celtic Consciousness.* New York: George Braziller, 1982.

Scully, Nicki. *Alchemical Healing: A Guide to Spiritual, Physical, and Transformational Medicine.* Rochester, VT: Bear and Company, 2003.

———. *Power Animal Meditations.* Rochester, VT: Bear and Company, 1991, 2001.

Scully, Nicki, and Linda Star Wolf. *Shamanic Mysteries of Egypt, Awakening the Healing Power of the Heart.* Rochester, VT: Bear & Company, 2007.

Scully, Nicki, and Linda Star Wolf. *The Anubis Oracle: A Journey into the Shamanic Mysteries of Egypt.* Rochester, VT: Bear & Company, 2008.

Starhawk. *Dreaming the Dark: Magic, Sex, and Politics.* Boston: Beacon Press, 1982.

———. *The Spiral Dance: A Rebirth of the Ancient Religion of the Great Goddess.* San Francisco: Harper and Row, 1979.

Starhawk, and M. Macha Nightmare. *The Pagan Book of Living and Dying: Practical Rituals, Prayers, Blessings, and Meditations on Crossing Over.* San Francisco: Harper, 1995.

Stein, Diane. *Casting the Circle: A Women's Book of Ritual.* Freedom, CA: The Crossing Press, 1990.

———. *Dreaming the Past, Dreaming the Future: A Herstory of the Earth*. Freedom, CA: The Crossing Press, 1991.

———. *Stroking the Python: Women's Psychic Lives*. St. Paul, MN: Llewellyn Publications, 1988.

Walker, Barbara G. *Women's Rituals: A Sourcebook*. San Francisco: Harper, 1990.

Weinstein, Marion. *Earth Magic: A Dianic Book of Shadows*. Custer, WA: Phoenix Publishing Inc., 1986.

Wilde, Lyn Webster. *Becoming the Enchanter: A Journey to the Heart of the Celtic Mysteries*. New York: Penguin Putnam Inc., 2002.